THE WILL
AND
THE WAY

CFI's office building in Raleigh at 2100 Yonkers Road near the Beltline and U.S. 1 North was occupied on March 21, 1988. The CFI Board of Trustees has named it the Victor E. Bell, Jr. Building in honor of Mr. Bell's more than 25 years of service as Chairman of the Board.

THE WILL
AND
THE WAY

A History of College Foundation Inc.
and the
North Carolina Insured Student Loan Program

By

T. HARRY GATTON

Published by the College Foundation Inc.
Raleigh, North Carolina
1989

First Edition
Copyright © 1989
All Rights Reserved
College Foundation Inc.
2100 Yonkers Road
Raleigh, North Carolina 27604

Library of Congress Catalogue Card Number 89-85681
International Standard Book Number
0-9624196-0-5 (Regular Edition)
0-9624196-1-3 (Special Edition)

Printed in the United States of America by
Theo Davis Sons, Inc.
Zebulon, North Carolina 27597

DEDICATION

This history of College Foundation Inc. is dedicated to the North Carolina Bankers Association Student Loan Committee, North Carolina banks and bankers for their cooperation and support in funding educational loans through the Foundation for over a quarter of a century, 1963 through 1989.

Victor E. Bell, Jr., CFI chairman of the board and chief executive officer

Duffy L. Paul, CFI president and chief staff executive

CONTENTS

Introduction

Student financial assistance has been a significant factor in breaking the cycle of poverty for many North Carolinians. More than 169,000 students have received financial assistance through College Foundation Inc.

North Carolina banks have provided the capital needed for student loans from $90,000 in 1963-64 to more than $50,000,000 in each of the past five years, 1984-89, first under the North Carolina Bankers Student Loan Plan, 1963-66, and then under the North Carolina Insured Student Loan Program from 1966 to the present.

The North Carolina State Education Assistance Authority has had an active role in the growth of the Foundation's programs of loans and grants by insuring the loans against death, disability and default, providing loan monies from the sale of revenue bonds and from earnings of the State Escheat Fund and grant funds from state appropriations to match federal dollars for Student Incentive Grants.

The Foundation has seen a tremendous growth from its modest beginning in 1955 with assets of $89,000 provided from funds raised by Governor Luther Hodges for the Business Development Corporation of North Carolina and the Research Triangle Park to its present ability to help thousands of students each year, from 200 in 1963-64 to over 30,000 in each of the past five years. This growth was fostered under the leadership of Victor E. Bell, Jr., as Chairman of the Board from 1962 to the present, along with other dedicated trustees, donors, special investors, staff, financial aid administrators, and many others.

In that tradition, College Foundation Inc., after over three decades of service to North Carolina, pledges its best efforts to continue to serve the young people of North Carolina and the economic life of our State well into the 21st century.

Duffy L. Paul
President and
Chief Staff Executive
College Foundation Inc.

Acknowledgements

Research for this manuscript jogged many memories of the founding and expansion of an organization that has been significant to higher education in North Carolina.

Student loans and how to finance them was a growing issue in 1955. College Foundation Inc., promoted by Governor Luther H. Hodges at that time during his feverish activity to increase business and industry in the State, at first did not appear to be a major player in the development of student loans. But the beginning mechanism was created in 1955. With the advent of the administration of Governor Terry Sanford in 1961, the assets of the fairly inactive CFI totaled $89,000.

What could be done?

Working with the North Carolina Bankers Association through its Student Loan Committee headed by Victor E. Bell, Jr., CFI was restructured in 1962 to provide a more viable funding mechanism for student loans. Mr. Bell was elected CFI chairman and has continued in that capacity to the present, giving more than a quarter of a century of helping to nurture CFI to its present peak of success, a notable public service contribution marked by its effectiveness and dedication.

There is no way for me to adequately express my appreciation to Chairman Bell, President Paul, the officers, trustees and staff, along with Stan Broadway, executive director of the North Carolina State Education Assistance Authority, and Al Fuqua, my successor as executive vice president of the North Carolina Bankers Association, Kenneth Wooten, Raleigh attorney, and State Treasurer Harlan Boyles.

This manuscript is a modest chronicle of the impressive record of the Foundation, its leaders and its supporters — especially the banks of North Carolina — that have funded the loan program for over 25 years.

CFI is positive evidence of a good idea fulfilled — student loans for North Carolinians — an investment in the future of the State of North Carolina.

T. Harry Gatton
Executive Vice President
(Retired)
North Carolina Bankers
Association

Incorporators of College Foundation
November 1955

Governor Luther H. Hodges

State Treasurer Edwin Gill

State Board of Higher Education
Chairman D. Hiden Ramsey

Chapter One

The Seed of an Idea — Governor Luther H. Hodges

Yet, I am reluctant to give up the ghost.
—GOVERNOR LUTHER H. HODGES
to Gregory Poole, College Foundation
Board, February 8, 1960

THE MANTLE OF GUBERNATOR-
IAL LEADERSHIP fell suddenly on Lieutenant Governor Luther Hartwell Hodges,
56, with the unexpected death on November 7, 1954, of Governor William Bradley
Umstead.

Umstead and Hodges had taken their
offices in January 1953, at a time when
North Carolina faced mounting problems.
Hodges, a successful former textile executive, sought to improve conditions through
industrialization. One of his proposals was
the organization of the Business Development Corporation (BDC) to help establish
new industries by making loans from funds
provided from the sale of stock. Prospective
stockholders were bankers, financiers, and
businessmen with whom the new chief
executive had a natural rapport before his
retirement in 1950 as vice president of
Marshall Field in New York City. He returned to North Carolina to enter the pri-
mary for lieutenant governor in 1952.

Chartered by the General Assembly in
1955, the BDC received a generally favorable response. The North Carolina Bankers
Association (NCBA), whose membership
included all of the commercial banks in
North Carolina, was a principal advocate of
the plan, and sent its then managing officer,

Jesse Helms, later United States Senator,
around the state to "sell" banker participation. This support provided a good basis for
the Hodges program.

Governor Hodges addressed the 1955
NCBA convention in Pinehurst on May 9.
He laid out the proposal for the BDC and
sought endorsement of the plan.

"I would be very grateful if that endorsement could be given at this convention," Hodges said.

Bankers were keenly aware of the
need for development in North Carolina.
They supported the principle of BDC.

Although support for the new enterprise
was pleasing, not everyone wished to buy
stock in BDC. They sought a way to make a
tax deductible contribution rather than
stock shares. Hodges was not a person to
easily "give up the ghost" about a good idea
to advance North Carolina.

The BDC launched a successful program. But what about those who wanted to
make a contribution rather than to purchase
stock?

Why not create a foundation for scholarships for North Carolina students?

This concept produced contributions
with the help of several prominent financial
and industrial leaders.

1

The College Foundation (CFI) was incorporated on November 29, 1955, chartered by Governor Hodges, State Treasurer Edwin Gill, and D. Hiden Ramsey, of Asheville, chairman of the North Carolina Board of Higher Education.

CFI began with total assets of $89,000, funds raised by Hodges while he was soliciting friends for the BDC. The first major contribution, $50,000, was made by R.J. Reynolds Tobacco Company.

The incorporators — Hodges, Gill and Ramsey — were joined by other corporate members in calling for an organizational meeting of CFI, set for 11 a.m., May 9, 1956, in the office of Governor Hodges. Other corporate members were Miles J. Smith, Sr., of Salisbury, vice chairman of the Board of Conservation and Development, and John P. Stedman, a Lumberton banker and chairman of the Business Development Corporation.

Hodges was elected temporary chairman. He presented to the first meeting of

J. Gregory Poole

CFI a copy of the certificate of incorporation. He announced that the original had been filed with Secretary of State Thad Eure and that a certified copy would be recorded in the office of the Clerk of Superior Court of Wake County. The bylaws were read and adopted. Governor Hodges was elected first president of CFI; Treasurer Gill, secretary. Hodges voted the proxies of Ramsey, Smith and Stedman.

Early members of the CFI board of trustees were Leonard Powers, Raleigh; William Long, Tarboro; Phil Whitley, Wendell; Reid Thompson, Raleigh; R. Mayne Albright, Raleigh; Mrs. Roland McClamroch, Sr., Chapel Hill; L.H. Jobe, Raleigh; J. Gregory Poole, Raleigh; Terry Sanford, Fayetteville; and Spencer Love, Greensboro. Sanford, an attorney and state legislator, was destined to play a major role later in the development of CFI.

The first meeting of the board of trustees was held in the Governor's Office on July 19, 1956. Present were Powers, Long, Poole, Sanford, Albright, McClamroch, and Jobe.

Powers was elected temporary chairman of the meeting.

Gregory Poole, a Raleigh businessman, was elected president; William Long, Tarboro manufacturer, vice president; and Leonard Powers, Raleigh attorney, secretary-treasurer.

At the meeting the following members of the CFI trustees were elected and their terms of office set:

Leonard Powers, Raleigh, 2 years
William R. (Bill) Long, Tarboro, 1 year
Gregory Poole, Raleigh, 2 years
Terry Sanford, Fayetteville, 1 year
R. Mayne Albright, Raleigh, 3 years
Mrs. Roland McClamroch, Sr.,
    Chapel Hill, 3 years
L. H. Jobe, Raleigh, 4 years

In CFI's first brochure, mailed shortly after its organization, Hodges, Gill and Ramsey promoted contributions. Sent "to a limited number of North Carolinians with a definite plea for your cooperation," CFI was described as "An Agency for Promoting an Increased Flow of Technically Trained

Personnel Essential to a Productive State and Nation." Directed mostly to North Carolina corporations, the brochure noted that "It is neither possible nor desirable for such an undertaking to be financed wholly by taxation," and pointed out that "The preservation of free enterprise in our modern world requires strong cooperation between business and our educational forces for training of those who are to continue its operation."

The second trustee meeting was held on December 3, 1956. A general solicitation program was approved. J. Spencer Love of Greensboro was elected to a two-year term on the board.

At the third meeting on May 6, 1957, Albright was elected secretary to succeed Powers, who resigned on May 6, 1957.

President Poole appointed a scholarship committee, consisting of Trustees Albright, McClamroch and Jobe, to make a study and report plans to award scholarships, as the trustees decided that at least one scholarship would be awarded "this year." That was accomplished. Three students were awarded $250 scholarships — one attending the University of North Carolina, and two at North Carolina State College.

The mechanism established to award scholarships was to permit the North Carolina Academy of Science to recommend students to CFI. Thirty-nine scholarships were awarded from 1957 to 1961, totaling $13,000.

Contributions under the early procedures were not sufficient to meet the demand. Several trustees expressed concern over the lack of funds to make a dent in the growing need. President Poole reported in September 1958 that a conference had been held prior to the annual meeting of the trustees concerning the future of CFI "to determine whether there were recommendations from the Governor or his office concerning the future program of College Foundation Inc." Attending that meeting were Poole and Albright, representing the Foundation, and Paul Johnston and Robert Giles of the staff

of Governor Hodges. The consensus was that the program should continue the same, at least until the next annual meeting "during which time further thought should be given to the possibility of closer coordination with, and perhaps administration of the Foundation affairs through, other scholarship programs of educational facilities of the state."

CFI's assets as of July 31, 1958, totaled $69,206.51.

As mentioned earlier, the first large contribution to CFI was made by R.J. Reynolds Tobacco Company. On December 21, 1955 — three weeks after CFI was chartered — Governor Hodges wrote to Robert M. Hanes, Winston-Salem banker. "I am glad that you are going to be able to help get donations to the College Foundation," he said. He pointed out that the Revenue Commissoner (then Eugene Shaw of Greensboro) had ruled them deductible. Hanes, a former legislator and former president of the American Bankers Association, as well as the North Carolina Bankers Association, understood as well as anyone the fine art of raising funds as shown by a letter from John C. Whitaker, chairman of the board of RJR. "Dear Rob," he wrote, "In response to your request of December 23 [1955] that our Company make a donation to College Foundation, Inc., the Executive Committee today voted to contribute $50,000 to this Foundation . . . ."

Trustee Albright found it necessary to resign. He did so by letter to Governor Hodges on February 19, 1960. He was a strong supporter of more funds to "assure a college education in business and science."

Hodges wrote to CFI President Poole on February 8, 1960, that he appreciated the feeling of the trustees that CFI "does not have very good prospects. Yet, I am reluctant to give up the ghost. I think there is a real need in this State for a general scholarhsip fund, not directly related to any particular college or university, which could support a substantial number of fairly modest scholarships on a merit and need basis, to be available to high school graduates residing in the State for attendance at any accredited private or public college in the State," he believed. He did not conclude to stop the organization, Hodges stated emphatically. He wanted all trustees to continue the study of various possibilities.

Trustee J. Spencer Love had shared information with Albright in 1959 that "Recently up at Harvard a group of people have been discussing expanding scholarship or loan funds by using some fairly small capital base for forming a company to make loans, and then borrowing from banks, rediscounting such loans to expand activities. Perhaps something along this line could be considered, thus broadening substantially the good that could be accomplished from a relatively limited amount of money," the Greensboro textile executive wrote.

Also, the trustees, at a meeting on October 13, 1959, had resolved: "Whereas, our experience as Trustees since 1956 indicates that further solicitation of funds is impracticable; and that the present funds and the annual awarding of scholarships from the Foundation income does not require a Board of Trustees such as now constituted . . . we respectfully recommend to the Governor 1) That we nominate a new Board of Trustees of persons professionally engaged in education work; or 2) That College Foundation, Inc. be dissolved and all assets be paid over to one or more educational institutions as provided in Article 3 of the Certificate of Incorporation."

This resolution apparently led Hodges to keep up the study for viable possibilities.

Who first suggested the idea of College Foundation?

Governor Hodges, of course, had frequent contact with the leadership of education, finance, business and industry. He used these contacts as idea sources and reactors to his many and diverse suggestions to develop North Carolina on a broad front. Some of these citizens he named as trustees of CFI. Others, such as Capus Waynick of High Point and W. Trent Ragland of Raleigh, were involved in the formation of CFI. For example, Hodges wrote a note to Ragland, January 6, 1956, saying, "A suggestion you made to Capus Waynick some months ago has resulted in the chartering of the College Foundation, Incorporated. I am writing you to become one of the first contributors to this Foundation. The methods of its operation and its objectives are set forth in the accompanying folder. Since they are consistent with your original suggestions, I know that the movement will have your substantial contribution." Apparently Waynick had suggested contents of the letter from Hodges to Ragland.

The Foundation board of trustees had six members in 1960: J. Gregory Poole, William R. Long, J. Spencer Love, Mrs. Roland McClamroch, and L.H. Jobe. Terry Sanford had launched his campaign to succeed Governor Hodges in 1961. If successful, Sanford had experience on the CFI board that could steer his decisions.

Governor Hodges set many records. He had served as chief executive longer than any other governor in the history of North Carolina since it became a state — 1954-1961. That was before the change to a limit of two four-year terms. He immediately became Secretary of Commerce in the administration of John F. Kennedy and later returned to the state to a leadership role in the Research Triangle Park of which he was a foremost advocate as governor.

Edward L. Rankin, private secretary to Governor Hodges, recalls his dedication to an idea and his insistence that study and hard work be guides to success. He did not let a project drop.

He is remembered for many significant accomplishments, including the fruition of the idea of the College Foundation.

Chapter Two

The Need Cited and the Program Structured — Governor Terry Sanford and the North Carolina Banks

You may recall that in Governor Sanford's recent television appearance, he invited students who are serious about going to college and who have problems to write him. Many have in fact written him.

—WILLIAM C. ARCHIE,
director, North Carolina Board of
Higher Education, and CFI trustee,
June 15, 1962

SINCE HIS YOUTH Terry Sanford, a Laurinburg native, had an idea of becoming governor of the Tar Heel State. His dream became a reality when he was inaugurated on January 5, 1961.

"The hopes of North Carolina, the hopes of America and the hopes of our world will rise higher from the desks of the classroom than from the launching pads at Cape Canaveral," he said. There was no doubt that he would put education as one of his major goals.

By the time of Sanford's inauguration, CFI was largely inactive. With his interest in education and with a twist of fate (an extemporaneous comment on a TV program), it seemed natural that Governor Sanford would turn to CFI in his interest in creating a low-cost student loan program. He remembered his experience as a CFI trustee.

What to do with the $85,000 in College Foundation's account was an appropriate question.

The News and Observer carried a story under two-column headlines on March 23, 1962:

Governor Terry Sanford

State Has $85,000
Unused School Fund

"What do you do when an $85,000 higher education fund which has escaped public attention suddenly falls into your lap?

"It is a question State government officials are finding hard to answer."

The article described the College Foundation. CFI's charter permitted trustees to select their successors, but vacancies had not been filled. The board of trustees had been reduced to only four — Sanford and Albright had resigned; J. Spencer Love had died. The four surviving trustees were J. Gregory Poole, William Long, Mrs. Roland McClamroch and L.H. Jobe.

"At present, State officials simply do not know what to do with the money," the article pointed out.

The wheels began to turn.

On May 16, 1962, Sanford wrote letters to a list of prominent bankers and educators, stating the student loan problem. "In response to a casual suggestion on a television program, I have received about one hundred inquiries . . . . " He referred to the financial problem prohibiting college attendance and "the inability of some capable students to obtain a single dollar during the freshman year."

Governor Sanford's meeting invitation was for May 22, 1962, in his office. The mailing list included: Lewis R. Holding, Raleigh; Carl McCraw, Charlotte; J.E. Paschall, Wilson; Addison Reese, Charlotte; Victor E. Bell, Jr., Raleigh; W.J. Smith, Charlotte; C.M. Allred, Raleigh; Oscar J. Mooneyham, Sr. (president of the North Carolina Bankers Association), Forest City; R.G. Page, Winston Salem; James H. Styers, Winston-Salem; William Archie, Raleigh; Edwin S. Lanier, Chapel Hill; Raymond A. Stone, Raleigh; Clifton T. Edwards, Raleigh; Budd E. Smith, Wingate; Rudolph Jones, Fayetteville; Leo W. Jenkins, Greenville; Lewis C. Dowdy, Greensboro; James H. Tucker, Greenville; Julian Mason, Chapel Hill; and Kenneth D. Raab, Raleigh.

CFI Chairman Victor E. Bell, Jr., recalls receiving an invitation to attend the meeting, and shortly thereafter was elected head of CFI, a position he still holds as chairman, 27 years of service, a remarkable record.

The Sanford appointments, called the College Loan Committee, met in Raleigh on August 3, 1962, with Chairman Bell.

The board of trustees of CFI met on July 12, 1962, with Poole, Long, Jobe and Mrs. McClamroch present. Additional trustees were elected: Victor E. Bell, Jr., Raleigh banker; Dr. William C. Archie, director, North Carolina Board of Higher Education; and Dr. Raymond A. Stone, Governor Sanford's representative on the North Carolina Curriculum Study, State Board of Education, Raleigh.

The reconstituted board convened on July 25 in Sanford's office. J. Gregory Poole presided. Victor E. Bell, Jr. was elected president; W. R. Long, vice president; and William C. Archie, secretary-treasurer.

The trustees voted approval of the scholarship program of the past, but agreed that "the future program of the Foundation be committed to a student loan fund program."

Bell reviewed the proposed plan for making loans to first-year college students and the participation of the banks in the plan. Howard Boozer and Kenneth Batchelor from the Board of Higher Education staff reported facts concerning applications for financial aid.

Boozer said that more than 1,000 application letters had been received by Governor Sanford. The Board of Higher Education had responded to each application, advising these prospective students how to proceed in obtaining such aid.

The trustees decided that CFI funds would be made available to students, subject to certain qualifications as determined by the trustees. The basic provisions included loans for high school graduates who lived in North Carolina and were entering as freshmen in a standard collegiate program in a college in North Carolina. The maximum loan amount was set at $500 per annum; loans were to bear interest at five percent per annum. When matured, they were to be repaid to the Foundation ninety days after graduation or termination, whichever was first.

To get the bankers fully involved, NCBA President Mooneyham appointed a Special Student Loan Committee, named CFI President Bell to head it. Members included R.G. Page, Jr., Winston-Salem; C.M. Allred, Raleigh; William P. Dyer III, Charlotte; Garland Johnson, Elkin; Robert Guy, Newland; E.D. Gaskins, Monroe; C.A. Poole, Hickory; Bowen Ross, Raleigh; Norris L. Hodgkins, Jr., Southern Pines; E.G. Thompson, Warsaw; Paul Wright, Jr., Durham; and Harry Gatton, NCBA managing officer, Raleigh. This NCBA committee has continued in existence to the present time. Its function has been essential to the success of CFI and the North Carolina Student Loan Program.

Governor Sanford's announcement about financial assistance continued to be broadcast in July and August, bringing in a total of 1,600 requests, according to Bell. The executive committee of the NCBA made a critical decision for student loans when it endorsed the student loan plan in principle. Quick action was urgent to structure the plan in final form for consideration by the NCBA's policy-making committee.

The pilot study for the development of student loans was done by Bell and R.G. (Dick) Page, Jr., Winston-Salem; W.P. Dyer III, Charlotte; Thornton B. (Ted) Morris and C.M. Allred, Raleigh.

Moving quickly, the plan was developed and ready for Bell's disclosure to the NCBA Student Loan Committee on September 27, 1962.

Meeting on October 18, 1962, that committee "unanimously and enthusiastically approved a plan which provides an opportunity for the banks of North Carolina to participate in enabling deserving students to acquire a college education," the NCBA informed its members. Said President Mooneyham, "This plan was approved after study and recommendation by a special Committee of the association, headed by Victor E. Bell, Jr., of Raleigh."

The NCBA president said that a public announcement of the plan would be on December 4, 1962, "after a majority of the North Carolina banks have agreed to participate in filling this challenging need and at the same time realizing overwhelming public support for developing North Carolina's youth." He urged all banks to participate.

Chairman Bell launched an intensive program of personal contact with the bankers. It was almost a full-time commitment that he made to enroll the banks.

After the approval by the NCBA Executive Committee on October 18, 1962, the NCBA's Public Relations and Marketing Committee, headed by D. Vernon Deal of North Wilkesboro, met and set in motion plans and details for the promotion of the Student Loan Plan. James W. Reid and Norwood W. (Red) Pope, Jr., Raleigh bankers, were named as a subcommittee to work out the details of specific promotion plans. Assisting Reid and Pope was Michael J. Silver, Raleigh advertising executive. Kits were prepared for total media coverage to be released on December 4.

The plan's provisions were explained in detail to the bankers of North Carolina.

What were they?

Bankers were informed by the NCBA: "Under the plan approved by the Association, a non-stock, non-profit corporation known as College Foundation, Incorporated, will administer the plan and handle all of the details of making and collecting loans to North Carolina high school graduates for the purpose of attending college in North Carolina. The plan will be known as the North Carolina Bankers Student Loan Plan. It is anticipated that the adoption of the plan will be a very valuable addition to the public relations of participating banks. There will be widespread distribution of information to the press and radio in order that banks will receive due recognition in connection with this plan.

"In order to participate in the plan, a bank must agree to lend up to one percent of its capital and surplus to the Foundation. Participating banks will be called upon on the line of credit from time to time as funds are needed and each participating bank will be called upon to lend a pro-rata share of the needed funds. From this money, the Foundation will make loans to students."

Chairman Bell gave the banks additional information, including the arrangement for guarantee of funds and word that the "legal soundness of the corporate structure of College Foundation, Incorporated has been approved by the North Carolina Bankers Association's General Counsel, James H. Pou Bailey, Raleigh attorney."

The "supersalesman" efforts by Chairman Bell to sign up the banks were quickly evident. Bankers recognized the "good purpose" nature of student loans. The NCBA leadership supported the program, and student loan experts were convinced that North Carolina had developed a program unique in the nation.

Bankers did not want to miss this opportunity for a great forward step in service.

NORTH CAROLINA BANKERS' STUDENT LOAN PLAN ✷ PRESS KIT

On Friday, November 30, 1962, the North Carolina Bankers Association mailed to each of the 100 County Key Bankers press kits marked "hold for release on December 4." They contained stories, audio tapes and films. The careful planning and distribution assured the print and broadcast media of timely material for use in connection with the formal announcement on Tuesday, December 4, 1962.

Chapter Three

Participation and Fanfare at the Mansion — The Will and the Way Announced

To the credit of the banks, they accepted the challenge and came up with a plan that probably goes beyond what even the government had dared expect.
—Editorial from *The Raleigh Times*, December 6, 1962

TUESDAY MORNING, DECEMBER 4, 1962 began as a showery day in Raleigh.

The Executive Mansion at 200 Blount Street, being prepared for the coming Christmas Season, stood in its Victorian elegance as bankers, educators, student loan administrators and the press assembled at noon for a buffet luncheon and important announcement about a student loan plan that was being launched.

The College Foundation, now with a revived vigor made possible by the bankers of North Carolina, stood on the threshold of a great challenge to administer student loans through funds made available from the banks.

Over 200 bankers and educators —and a large number of reporters of the print and electronic media — heard the news of the North Carolina Bankers Student Loan Plan, made by Governor Sanford and NCBA President Oscar J. Mooneyham, Sr. Chairman Bell, head of the NCBA Student Loan Committee and CFI, reported that 97 banks had volunteered to participate in the new plan. The home-developed plan was launched as a major effort to develop the state's human resources.

To make the plan feasible, the participating banks agreed to lend up to one per-

cent of their capital and surplus to the College Foundation. The banks provided the funds; students, working with student aid officers of the colleges and universities of the state, would submit their loan applications to CFI, the nonprofit agency created to administer the loans.

In making the announcement at the Executive Mansion luncheon, Governor Sanford offered his full support to the new college loan plan.

"Everyone in this state shares a concern for the future of education and especially higher education," he said. "And this year thousands of letters have come to my office from young people who have the ability . . . and have the desire to go to college but do not have adequate finances," he reported.

"Today, I'm happy to tell you that this problem will be met — largely through the efforts of the bankers of North Carolina who have for some time been working on a Student Loan Plan," Sanford concluded.

Media coverage was extensive.

Said Chairman Bell, "Public response to the North Carolina Bankers Student Loan Plan has been wonderful. Many bankers tell me that the inquiries have been tremendous."

9

"If you have the will and the skill, we will help you go to college," Governor Sanford told high school graduates on a statewide television broadcast in June 1962.

With the provision for student loans, announced on December 4, 1962, the third leg of the program — the way — was added to the will and the skill.

Few of the large crowd at the Executive Mansion that December day in 1962 could have envisioned the impact the Bankers Student Loan Plan would have and its value to thousands of North Carolinians. It was generally believed that a $5 million revolving loan fund would meet the needs of North Carolina's students. Little did anyone realize then that annual lending would reach $50 million or more within two decades.

Noted *The Tarheel Banker*, "Congratulations to the many faithful people who have worked tirelessly to nurture this idea to fruition. They are bankers of vision, unselfish in their devotion to organized banking and the work of the North Carolina Bankers Association. Let their work be long remembered."

Chapter Four

On the Way — College Foundation in Action

Education is learning what you didn't even know you didn't know.
—Ralph Waldo Emerson

THE COLLEGE FOUNDATION, incorporated in 1955, was organized as a scholarship fund.

In 1962, under the leadership of Governor Sanford, the CFI charter was amended to make the assets of the Foundation available as a loan fund.

Formal announcement of the revived College Foundation was distributed by news dispatches from Raleigh on August 21, 1962. The stories said: "A new organization has been set up aimed at helping

At a luncheon at the Executive Mansion in Raleigh on December 4, 1962, the significant announcement of the creation of the North Carolina Bankers Student Loan Fund was made by Governor Sanford (center), Victor E. Bell, Jr., chairman of the NCBA Student Loan Committee, and NCBA President Oscar J. Mooneyham, Sr.

qualified students who lack funds necessary to get into college."

The report noted that a very small amount of funds would be available in the fall, and the amount would be limited to $500 and only to entering college freshman. The interest rate was five percent.

Applications for student loans began, but it was clear that additional funds would be needed.

How could this be done?

The answer was to start with the bankers of North Carolina.

But it was reasonable that banks would not invest on a very large scale until there was a mechanism for their involvement in the policy-making of CFI.

This was quickly resolved by Chairman Bell, Joel Fleishman of Governor Sanford's office, and James H. Pou Bailey, general counsel of the North Carolina Bankers Association. On October 11, 1962, Attorney Bailey reported to the NCBA that the final draft of the amended CFI charter had been completed. This included the provision that four of the seven trustees were to be appointed by the Governor of North Carolina from a list of active bankers submitted by the North Carolina Bankers Association. Bailey recommended approval of the revised charter.

The bankers approved, believing that CFI would be able to operate a sound business organization that would enhance banker participation.

From a list of bankers recommended by the NCBA, four were selected by Governor Sanford: Victor E. Bell, Jr., Raleigh, who was a trustee and president of CFI, before the revised charter; W.L. Burns, Jr., Durham; R.G. Page, Jr., Winston-Salem, also a continuing member; and Norris L. Hodgkins, Jr., Southern Pines, who was president of the NCBA Young Bankers Division. The three non-bankers named were: William Archie, director of the Board of Higher Education, Raleigh; Raymond Stone, head of Curriculum Studies of the North Carolina Department of Education, Raleigh; and Frank H. Kenan, Durham businessman. Archie and Stone were also members of the old board.

The trustees met for the first time under the revised charter on January 15, 1963, in the board room of First Citizens Bank in Raleigh. Also present were attorneys Joel Fleishman, James H. Pou Bailey, and George R. Ragsdale.

Bell, who had held the office of president since July 25, 1962, was elected chairman and chief executive officer, the title changed by the revised charter. Burns was elected vice chairman; and Dr. Archie, treasurer and temporary secretary.

A statement of lending policies and a proposed form of agreement between CFI and participating colleges and universities were tentatively approved.

Attorney Bailey was requested to draw up a set of bylaws for CFI to be considered at the next meeting of the trustees.

That meeting, February 15, 1963, transacted the proper business of CFI:
- Adopted the bylaws and seal of the corporation.
- Adopted the loan policy.
- Authorized the execution of contracts with North Carolina banks.
- Approved a contract form for use with colleges and universities.
- Approved a Student Application for Loan from CFI.
- Approved the financial report.
- Voted to continue using Attorney

Attorney James H. Pou Bailey

James H. Pou Bailey as acting secretary and general counsel of the corporation.
- Authorized Dr. William Archie and Dr. Raymond Stone to study personnel requirements and to make recommendations to the Executive Committee.

With the new emphasis and increasing activity, the necessity for a staffed office was obvious. A search committee consisting of Dr. Archie and Chairman Bell recommended the election of Stan C. Broadway as executive secretary. Broadway was director of admissions and financial aid at High Point College, High Point.

Chairman Bell announced that Broadway would begin his duties effective June 3, 1963. He was welcomed to the full meeting of the trustees on June 13, at which time he was also appointed corporate secretary.

Efforts were being planned to launch a campaign for increased capital funds. The board agreed to use CFI's capital funds until $50,000 in loans had been accumulated. At that time, a call was to be made for loan funds to the participating banks.

Among Broadway's first duties were those of making the best use of CFI's loan assets in the late summer of 1963. School for the 1963-64 year would soon begin. An extensive tour of every North Carolina college was immediately begun to acquaint the schools with the plans of the Foundation. Before the summer of 1963 was over, every college had been visited and 223 loans totaling $90,000 had been made to students who had no other source of funds to meet the costs of enrolling in the Fall of 1963.

As plans developed, CFI moved from the third floor to the tenth floor of First Citizens Bank Building in downtown Raleigh. The trustees set loan volume for freshmen in the 1964-65 year at up to $300,000.

Loans for the 1963-64 year had been made from the Foundation's assets in anticipation of a capital funds campaign. Carl Harris, a Durham textile executive, was asked to head the drive. Harris led a valiant effort, but the drive met with modest success. Capital funds were hard to secure; the $154,000 raised came at a critical time for CFI.

Broadway became concerned that funds for operating CFI might be inadequate to continue another year without adequate capital funds. He had been offered several administrative positions, and in 1964 he accepted a position with Wake Forest University in Winston-Salem to head their financial aid program.

The CFI trustees then turned to Duffy L. Paul, who had succeeded Broadway as financial aid director at High Point College, to succeed him as executive secretary, effective August 1, 1964. A native of Morehead City, Paul attended Louisburg and High Point colleges and obtained a master's degree in education at the University of North Carolina at Greensboro. He was unanimously recommended for the post by the Foundation's executive committee on July 6, 1964.

Funds from the original gifts to CFI

secured by Governor Hodges were available to form the base from which student loans were made to needy students in 1963.

As Paul has noted, "The College Foundation, Inc. proved to be invaluable when the committee of civic minded citizens appointed by Governor Sanford was seeking a mechanism to administer a proposed student loan plan.

"While the initial gift would not be sufficient to meet state-wide loan demands, it proved to be a base from which loans were made to needy students during the fall of 1963," he said.

Both Broadway and Paul salute the invaluable work of Victor E. Bell, Jr.

"Without a doubt, the name that looms largest on this early horizon is Victor E. Bell, Jr.," Broadway says. "His vision of what we wanted and needed to accomplish never faltered . . . . "

"The appointment of a dynamic and able Raleigh banker, Victor E. Bell, Jr., proved to be an outstanding choice," Paul comments. "With unmatched enthusiasm the bankers of North Carolina responded to Bell's call and eighty-five percent of the state's banks subscribed two and a half million dollars within thirty days," he notes.

In the beginning participating banks agreed to loan to CFI four dollars for every one dollar of the Foundation's assets.

In 1963 — two years before Congress authorized a broad spectrum of student financial assistance through Title IV of the Higher Education Act of 1965 — CFI was in the process of awarding $90,000 in student loans under the N.C. Bankers Student Loan Plan.

The first borrower from College Foundation in 1963 was Brenda Campbell Spivey of Rocky Mount.

She was graduated from Atlantic Christian College with a Bachelor's degree and a major in business administration.

"I was the baby of five children," she reports. "My parents couldn't afford college for any of us. Through loans and work I got through," she says.

CFI awarded 223 loans for the academic year 1963-64, averaging $390.

13

On September 1, 1964, CFI became the administrator of the student loan plan of the James E. and Mary Z. Bryan Foundation.

The promise and the fulfillment were on track. As was said, "This program is not a dream — it is a living, breathing reality."

CFI was in action and on the way.

But the demand for student loans mounted dramatically.

What about a marketable student loan revenue bond?

That answer was not easy coming.

Chapter Five

Private and Public — State Education Assistance Authority Created

The College Foundation is unique in the nation and its existence will help North Carolina students to take advantage immediately of the loan benefits available to them by the Higher Education Act of 1965.
—Governor Dan K. Moore, February 24, 1966

A GIANT FORWARD STEP was taken by the North Carolina General Assembly on June 17, 1965.

The Assembly had convened on February 3. Legislators were anxious to wind up the session. As the Senate and House were in the last hours before *sine die* adjournment on June 17, Senate Bill 531, providing for the creation of the State Education Assistance Authority (the Authority) was passed as amended by both houses and ratified.

Senator J. Russell Kirby of Wilson introduced the bill on June 3, 1965. It was referred to the Committee on Higher Education by Senate President Robert W. Scott. Heading that committee was Senator Ralph Scott of Haw River. Other members were Roy Rowe, Burgaw, vice chairman; Jack H. White, Kings Mountain, vice chairman; J. Ruffin Bailey, Raleigh; Irwin Belk, Charlotte; Mrs. Martha W. Evans, Charlotte; F.D.B. Harding, Yadkinville; Herbert L. Hyde, Old Fort; Walter B. Jones, Farmville;

State Senator J. Russell Kirby introduced the bill to create the State Education Assistance Authority.

Harlan E. Boyles, in 1965 State Treasurer Edwin Gill's chief deputy, and currently State Treasurer

J. Russell Kirby, Wilson; Don S. Matheson, Hillsboro; L.P. McLendon, Jr., Greensboro; Herman A. Moore, Charlotte; Lindsay C. Warren, Jr., Goldsboro; Thomas J. White, Kinston; and Sam L. Whitehurst, New Bern.

Senator Kirby's bill had the strong support of the North Carolina Bankers Association, the College Foundation, Governor Dan K. Moore, and State Treasurer Edwin Gill.

The present State Treasurer Harlan E. Boyles, who as Mr. Gill's chief deputy in 1965, remembers the remarkable unity in support of the measure in the Council of State. The main question, he recalls, was on perfecting the bill to be certain that it would meet any court challenge.

"There was no question on the merits of the bill," Boyles reports. He says the efforts of Victor E. Bell, Jr., CFI chairman, and Kenneth F. Wooten, Jr., Raleigh attorney, were invaluable in securing the enactment of the legislation.

Chairman Scott of the Senate Committee on Higher Education reported the bill favorably on June 11. On Monday, June 14, Senator Kirby, after input of the various supporters, amended the bill, and it passed the Senate on second and third readings.

The measure met a favorable vote in the House, and the bill was ratified on June 17, 1965, the 116th day of the session, signed into law by Senate President Robert W. Scott of Haw River and House Speaker H. P. Taylor, Jr., Wadesboro.

Governor Moore appointed the first seven members of the board of the Authority on January 1, 1966: H. Edmunds White, Davidson; Victor E. Bell, Jr., Raleigh; Mrs. Carrie W. Harper of Greensboro; George Watts Hill, Jr., Chapel Hill; J. Russell Kirby, Wilson; and Arthur D. Wenger of Wilson.

The principal purpose of the State Education Assistance Authority was to insure or guarantee student loans against loss to the investors who were providing the capital for the loans. It was recognized that for the student loan program to work

effectively, the State of North Carolina had to become more directly involved in the process.

Addressing the North Carolina Bankers Association convention in Pinehurst, May 10, 1965, CFI Chairman Bell recalled that the North Carolina Bankers Student Loan Plan was established in 1962 by ninety participating banks and that the College Foundation was named to administer the plan. He reported also that the first loans were made in the 1963-64 academic year and that since 1963 CFI had made loans to 485 students attending 43 colleges and universities in North Carolina totaling $195,000. The maximum amount that could be borrowed was $750, up from $500, Bell told the bankers.

"The need for student financial assistance in the form of loans will increase along with the increase in college admissions. Our concern is to encourage more North Carolina students that more funds would be needed," Bell said.

A major problem for CFI was that it insured the student loans with its own assets.

The State Education Assistance Authority was designed to serve as a guarantee agency for the loans. It maintains a Reserve Trust Fund to accomplish this.

CFI's trustees in 1966 expanded the Bankers Student Loan Plan to include provisions of Title IV of the Higher Education Act of 1965, which provided the low-interest long-term insured student loans with federal interest benefits for eligible lenders. CFI was designated an eligible lender by the U.S. Office of Education in 1966. Governor Moore sought and obtained the support of life insurance companies in North Carolina to become investors in the Insured Student Loan Program in 1966. He had worked closely with a Raleigh insurance company executive, Micou F. Browne, to secure the participation of life insurance companies in the student loan plan.

In a letter to officers of these North Carolina life insurance companies Browne wrote: "This overall program appears to be a real challenge to those of us in the private

16

sector to furnish insured, interest-bearing funds to deserving candidates for higher education." He noted that North Carolina Commissioner of Insurance Edwin S. Lanier had approved the program. He told Browne that his experience of 31 years as director of Student Financial Aid at the University of North Carolina at Chapel Hill led him to "believe fully in the wisdom and values of encouraging and aiding financially needy, capable, meritorious and determined young people to further their post high school education."

On August 30, 1966, Governor Moore announced that 12 North Carolina life insurance companies had agreed to participate in the student loan plan administered by CFI and insured by the Authority. The total amount of the participation over a four-year period would be $1,200,000 according to Duffy Paul of CFI. He noted in his report: "This action brought the Foundation's total line of credit with the banks and the life insurance companies to almost $5 million."

Governor Moore announced the details of the Higher Education Financial

In 1966, Governor Dan K. Moore by executive order designated the State Education Assistance Authority (SEAA) as the loan guarantee agency to enter into agreements with the U.S. Office of Education. Standing (left to right) are Victor E. Bell, Jr., chairman, CFI Board of Trustees; John Corey, State Board of Higher Education; Watts Hill, Jr., chairman, SEAA Board of Directors; Duffy L. Paul, CFI executive director; and Stan C. Broadway, SEAA executive director. Seated (left to right) are Harold McGee, U.S. Office of Education, and Governor Moore.

Assistance Program on February 24, 1966. He expressed appreciation to the private lenders who were cooperating in the College Foundation program. "Simply stated," he said, "the student loan program for North Carolina is one which will entitle almost any student to borrow up to $5,000 for undergraduate study or up to $7,500 for graduate work. The loan itself will be largely guaranteed by the State Education Assistance Authority," Governor Moore pointed out.

By executive order, he designated the State Board of Higher Education to be the host state agency for the State Education Assistance Authority and the Authority as the loan guarantee agency to enter into agreements with the U.S. Office of Education.

To keep the ball rolling with bankers, the NCBA's Public Relations and Public Education Committee, headed by A.H. (Art) Jones of Charlotte, held a Student Loan Workshop at the Velvet Cloak Inn, Raleigh, on August 4, 1966.

Micou F. Browne

Governor Moore was on hand to address the 164 bankers present. Said he, with television cameras grinding away, "We are grateful to the banks of North Carolina for making loan funds available through the College Foundation, which was established by forward-looking leaders several years ago. This enabled us to be among the first states to implement this new plan authorized by Federal law and legislation passed by the 1965 General Assembly."

Other speakers were Watts Hill, Jr., chairman of the Board of Higher Education and the State Education Assistance Authority; Dr. Kingston Johns, Jr., assistant director of the Southern Regional Office, College Entrance Examination Board; CFI Chairman Victor E. Bell, Jr.; Stan C. Broadway, executive director of the State Education Assistance Authority; and Duffy L. Paul, executive director of CFI.

Commented Chairman Jones, "A lot was done here today by very competent people who gave their time and talents to this important activity."

As the need for more student loan money increased, new and innovative funding mechanisms were sought.

Dick Page asked, "Why not create a marketable, tax-exempt bond to be issued by the State Education Assistance Authority?"

His idea fell on fertile soil.

On April 5, 1966, NCBA President Emsley A. Laney of Wilmington convened a special meeting of the NCBA executive committee in the Hotel Sir Walter in Raleigh. The chief purpose of the meeting was to discuss the College Foundation "and the increasing demands for student loan funds." He said the demand was so heavy that "the present system of participation by the banks in CFI was not adequate to meet the need."

President Laney reviewed the results of a meeting of the officers of the NCBA and trustees of CFI "at which time the problem was discussed thoroughly." He reported that he, Clyde Stutts, Shelby banker, and Harry Gatton, NCBA executive vice president, had met "this morning" with State Treasurer Edwin Gill and members of his staff, along with Wayne Corpening of Governor Moore's office, and that considerable interest was expressed in exploring the idea of tax-exempt revenue bonds as quickly as possible to see what could be done.

At the meeting strong support for the ideas was voiced. Attorney Kenneth Wooten reported on the legal technicalities and "indicated that he is of the opinion that the matter can be resolved favorably." He urged quick action. CFI Chairman Bell said the proposal "seems to be the only practical solution to derive the necessary student loan funds."

On motion of Clyde Stutts, seconded

R.G. Page, Jr.

Emsley A. Laney

Clyde L. Stutts

by Ralph B. Hunter of Broadway, the NCBA executive committee "gave its unanimous and whole-hearted support for the proposal and directed that it be pursued with vigor to see if such a plan can be accomplished."

President Laney told the executive committee at its meeting at the NCBA convention in Pinehurst on May 5, 1967, that he had named Clyde L. Stutts to head the effort for a student loan revenue bond, and that he was working with the Office of Governor, Office of Treasurer, and the Trustees of CFI and "that great progress has been made." Stutts, the immediate past president of the North Carolina Bankers Association (1965-66), was, along with others, a tireless worker for student loans.

The NCBA authorized the expenditure of up to $5,000 to help defray cost of developing a suitable bill to amend the statute of the State Education Assistance Authority to permit the issuance of revenue bonds.

The positive news came on June 26, 1967, when NCBA managing officer Harry Gatton notified all the bankers that "Senate Bill 738 has been introduced by Senator Lindsay C. Warren, Jr., of Wayne, and is before the Senate Calendar Committee. If enacted by the General Assembly, it will help provide urgently needed funds for student loans. It would permit banks, for example, to invest in tax-exempt securities for student loans.... SB 738 merits your immediate attention and support.... If adopted, this legislation will be a model for the nation.... It has the support of the Administration [Governor Dan K. Moore], Treasurer Edwin Gill, the State Education Assistance Authority, College Foundation, Inc., and the North Carolina Bankers Association."

The bill was reported favorably by unanimous action of the Senate Calendar Committee on June 30. Senator Warren asked Representative R.D. McMillan, Jr., of Robeson County, to lead the bill in the House Calendar Committee. There it met a favorable response. The bill was quickly passed and ratified.

With the Senate's passing the bill without any difficulty, all hands looked back to the meeting of March 30, 1967, in the NCBA board room as the officers and finance committee of the NCBA met with CFI's board of trustees and recommended to the executive committee "that they investigate the possibility of enabling legislation." NCBA Treasurer H.W. Safriet, Reidsville banker, chairman of the NCBA finance committee, made the motion, seconded by W.C. Barrett, Laurinburg, NCBA first vice president, an action that CFI trustees also supported. Attending that session from CFI were Chairman Bell; Raymond A. Stone, treasurer; Robert E. Bryan; R.G. Page, Jr.; William H. Stanley; Duffy L. Paul, executive director and secretary; Norman T. Watson, assistant director. From the NCBA were Emsley A. Laney, president; W.C. Barrett, first vice president; J. Paul Ford, second vice president; H.W. Safriet, treasurer; Robert P. Holding, Jr., NCBA president in 1964-65; and Harry Gatton, executive director.

The General Assembly acted on July 5, 1967, moving rapidly after its introduction in the Senate by Senator Warren on June 26.

NCBA managing officer Harry Gatton sent the following memo to the Special Student Loan Committee: "Congratulations! SB 738 passed both houses unanimously. House took final action today. Bill authorizes State Education Assistance Authority to issue up to $12½ million in tax-exempt bonds for student loan purposes. Special thanks to Chairman Clyde Stutts who headed the special committee and to Chairman Edwin Pate of the Legislative Committee who has devoted many hours of time to the Association's legislative program."

On August 2, 1967, Gatton wrote the committee that "Chairman Stutts, Ruffin Bailey, Kenneth Wooten, Duffy Paul, Victor E. Bell, Jr. and I met with Harlan Boyles, Watts Hill, Jr., Stan Broadway and Wayne Corpening in Raleigh last week to get a composite picture of the present situtation and thinking .... It was decided that the

[State] Education Assistance Authority would need a test case decision and that this will be pursued instantly." Bailey was NCBA general counsel and Wooten was of the same law firm in Raleigh. He led the legal planning for a test case.

At the 1967 NCBA convention CFI Chairman Bell reported that the Foundation had made over 1,500 educational loans, totaling approximately $500,000. "The trustees of College Foundation have been working closely with the officials of the Bankers Association in an effort to secure additional inducements in order that our lenders may make greater commitments to our student lending program."

The marketable tax-exempt revenue bond appeared to be the answer.

In 1968 Chairman Bell reported to the bankers that CFI had made 5,000 educational loans to North Carolina students attending 200 schools, totaling $3.2 million. The board of trustees of CFI had been increased from seven to nine members, with five members being active bankers.

"Our loan value is almost doubling each year," he said.

Participating banks could purchase the student loan revenue bonds from the State Education Assistance Authority in lieu of lending funds directly to CFI. CFI would continue to administer the North Carolina Insured Student Loan Plan under agreement with the State Education Assistance Authority.

Twelve life insurance companies and eight educational institutions joined in making loan funds available, Bell reported. Also, loans were being made to students attending colleges, universities, technical and vocational schools. The administrative staff of CFI, headed by Duffy Paul, numbered fourteen, up from two in 1963.

The late historian Hugh T. Lefler wrote, "Dan Moore came into office following a decade of dynamic gubernatorial leadership. Luther Hodges (1954-61) and Terry Sanford (1961-65) had set a fast pace.... In his quiet, unostentatious way he went about putting his program into effect."

Succeeding governors — Robert W. Scott, James E. Holshouser, James B. Hunt, Jr., and James E. Martin — named men and women of stature to the boards of CFI and the State Education Assistance Authority.

Stan C. Broadway, who was the first executive secretary of CFI, became executive director of the State Education Assistance Authority in 1966. He was succeeded in 1964 by Duffy L. Paul who has unbroken service to CFI and continues as president. Chairman Victor E. Bell, Jr., began his service in 1962 and continues to the present time in that office. Leading the SEAA have been these chairmen: Watts Hill, Jr., J. Russell Kirby, Ed Baker, Dick Futrell, and George Erath. The competence of leadership, support of student loans by the bankers and others, were essential factors in CFI's beginning and its continuation, along with the Authority.

In 1966 Terry Sanford in his book, *But What About the People?* told of the first funds obtained by Governor Hodges. He con-

Stan C. Broadway, first executive secretary of CFI (1963-64) and since 1966, executive director of the State Education Assistance Authority

tinued by writing that "we called upon the bankers to set up a loan program . . . and the bankers made several millions more available. . . . It is working out very well and will be expanded from year to year."

The North Carolina Association of Student Financial Aid Administrators on November 6, 1969, expressed "grateful appreciation to the College Foundation, Inc. and to participating North Carolina banks and life insurance companies for rendering exemplary service in furthering the cause of higher education in North Carolina."

Private and public cooperation — North Carolina's student loan program administered became the model for the nation. It has fit well into the Federal mosaic on student loans. The Tar Heel State had an operating and successful program before Washington took action.

There was one more bump in the road — the constitutionality of tax-exempt student loan revenue bonds.

Only the courts could settle that.

The State Education Assistance Authority issued revenue bonds to increase the amount of student loan money available. All of these bonds are now retired.

D2780

Nº

UNITED STATES OF AMERICA
STATE OF NORTH CAROLINA

STATE
EDUCATION
ASSISTANCE
AUTHORITY

$1000

5½%
STATE EDUCATION
ASSISTANCE AUTHORITY
REVENUE BOND, SERIES B

DATED JULY 1, 1969

PRINCIPAL DUE

JULY 1, 1989
Subject to Prior Redemption as Herein Provided

INTEREST PAYABLE
JANUARY 1 and JULY 1

SPECIMEN

PRINCIPAL AND INTEREST PAYABLE
AT THE PRINCIPAL OFFICE OF
WACHOVIA BANK AND TRUST
COMPANY, N.A.
IN THE CITY OF RALEIGH, NORTH CAROLINA
OR, AT THE OPTION OF THE HOLDER AT
BANKERS TRUST COMPANY
IN THE BOROUGH OF MANHATTAN
CITY AND STATE OF NEW YORK

SECURITY-COLUMBIAN BANKNOTE COMPANY

Chapter Six

Student Loan Revenue Bonds — the Courts Gave the Green Light

Having determined that Chapter 1177 does not violate any of the provisions of the State or Federal Constitutions referred to in the agreed state, the judgment of the court below is affirmed.

—Decision of the Supreme Court of North Carolina,
Chief Justice William H. Bobbitt, Spring Term 1970,
filed June 12, 1970

THE SIGNIFICANCE OF A COURT TEST on the constitutionality of the tax-exempt student loan revenue bonds issued by the State Education Assistance Authority was obvious.

Clyde L. Stutts of Shelby, chairman of the NCBA Student Loan Committee, and one of the leaders in promoting student loans, wrote on April 3, 1970: "We have received information from our counsel Bailey, Dixon, Wooten & McDonald, that this case will be heard by the Supreme Court on April 15, and let us hope for a prompt favorable decision in order that we might proceed with our plans. If we are not so fortunate, then this is entirely another ball game since our banks did make it entirely clear that they did not intend to purchase any more bonds until the constitutional question has been resolved."

On April 15, 1970, Attorney Kenneth Wooten, Jr. wrote Stutts that "The above captioned test case (State Education Assistance Authority v. Bank of Statesville) on the Series 'E' Student Loan Revenue Bonds of State Education Assistance Authority was argued this morning in the Supreme Court. The Court was very interested in the litigation, and I am hopeful from their

questions that we will soon have a decision on the constitutionality and legality of these bonds so that this program can move ahead."

Raleigh Attorney Kenneth Wooten, Jr., a leader for court approval of the student loan revenue bonds

22

In June 1969 CFI Chairman Bell told the bankers about the court proceedings. He recalled that in the fall of 1968, the Authority issued the first student loan revenue bonds authorized by the 1967 General Assembly (Chapter 1177). Participating banks, Bell noted, purchased the first issue of $3 million. He said that the Superior Court of Wake County had rendered a favorable opinion but that the decision had been appealed to the Supreme Court.

CFI's trustees met on February 17, 1970. CFI Executive Director Duffy L. Paul wrote to Harry Gatton, executive vice president of the NCBA, that Trustee R.G. Page, Jr., of Winston-Salem, a banker who helped develop the student loan program in the beginning, "suggested that the Bankers Association Student Loan Bond Committee continue its work concerning the design of a marketable student loan revenue bond." Continued Paul, "As you will recall, Mr. Robert Holding and Mr. Logan Pratt met with several others concerning this question and designed the revenue bonds which have been sold to date."

At the time the NCBA Student Loan Committee, appointed by President William H. Stanley of Rocky Mount, was Clyde L. Stutts, Shelby, chairman; Robert P. Holding, Jr., Smithfield; Foy N. Goforth, Wilson; James R. Sheridan, Charlotte; H.J. Runnion, Jr., Winston-Salem; and W.J. Smith, Charlotte.

In 1970 Goforth became a member of the CFI's board of trustees. He served on the board until 1987 and as vice chairman for a number of years. In 1976 Runnion joined the CFI board and continues to serve, currently as vice chairman.

To provide a court test, the Bank of Statesville agreed to be the defendant in the test. It did so by refusing to purchase revenue bonds issued by the State Education Assistance Authority "because it stated that it believed that there was a question as to the legal authority of the Authority to issue the bond and to comply with the contract."

Deputy Attorney General Harry W. McGalliard represented the Authority in the civil suit. Bank of Statesville was represented by Isaac T. Avery, Jr., Statesville, and Kenneth Wooten, Jr., Raleigh.

The critical test case was heard before Judge James H. Pou Bailey on February 9, 1969, in the Civil Term of Wake County Superior Court. On February 26, Judge Bailey ruled that the revenue bonds in question "have been duly and legally authorized

Foy N. Goforth and H.J. Runnion, Jr., members of the NCBA Student Loan Committee and later CFI trustees

23

and duly and legally sold to the Bank of Statesville . . . . "

Notice of appeal to the Supreme Court was given.

The Supreme Court affirmed the decision of Judge Bailey and "determined that Chapter 1177 does not violate any of the provision of the State or Federal Constitutions . . . . "

Another attorney, Joseph Guandolo, New York bond attorney for the Authority, worked closely with authorities to be certain that the student loan bonds would meet the test of a court case.

Attorney Ken Wooten recalls the close cooperation given to determine the validity of the revenue bonds. CFI was hard pressed for student loan fund money to take care of the growing demand for students for college funds.

Authority Chairman Watts Hill, Jr., Durham, noted in a newspaper feature in 1969 that "In the past few days there have been news reports of the very real difficulties which college students face this fall in financing their higher education."

Said Hill, "North Carolina has a unique program for making loans to students. This program was conceived by the bankers of the State. Over the years this program has made loans totaling $5,000,000 and this fall almost $2 million in new loans will be made through financial aid officers in the colleges by the College Foundation, Inc., acting for the state's banks and insurance companies . . . . The long term outlook for sufficient student financial aid is excellent. The short term prospects are not good," he said.

The student loan "crunch" resulted in ten banks being asked to underwrite the $1.5 million proposed bond issue.

The wisdom of the endorsement of revenue bonds by CFI and the NCBA, and approval by the State Education Assistance Authority, and the courts, put the student loan program on a more realistic basis through a marketable bond.

Chapter Seven

Expansion — Filling the Student Loan Needs

*Although student loans are high-risk, no investor
in the Bankers Plan or the Insured Loan Program
has experienced any loss.*

—DUFFY L. PAUL, CFI president, article in
The Tarheel Banker, November 1976

THE 1987-88 ANNUAL REPORT of College Foundation, Inc. was dedicated to present and past members of the North Carolina Bankers Association Student Loan Committee "for their cooperation in encouraging North Carolina full-service banks to fund educational loans through College Foundation, Inc. for twenty-five consecutive years, 1963-88."

Banks provided more than $400 million to make over 250,000 loans to more than 100,000 borrowers.

The Foundation, a North Carolina nonprofit corporation and a 501 (c) 3 private operating foundation under the Internal Revenue Code, administers three educational loan programs as North Carolina's central lender. The cooperative effort between the banks as the provider of funds, the State Education Assistance Authority as the state guaranty agency, and the U.S. Department of Education, which provides reinsurance and federal interest benefits forms a notable working arrangement. Insured Student Loans, Supplemental Loans for Students and PLUS Loans for parents provide over $50 million annually for North Carolina students attending colleges in and out of North Carolina.

In addition to the educational loan programs, CFI administers the Student Incentive Grant Program funded through the State Education Assistance Authority with state matching federal dollars, exceeding $3 million annually. The total amount of grants provided, 1975-88, is more than $36 million to over 40,000 students.

The report concluded: "In planning for the future of our student financial assistance programs, we recognize that our continued success in helping students pay their educational expenses depends on the continuing interest and support of participating banks, the State Education Assistance Authority, special investors, donors, trustees, staff, financial aid administrators, high school counselors, and many others."

Between 1968 and 1981, financing for the Insured Student Loan Program came primarily through the sale of tax-exempt revenue bonds. Because of the unstable tax-exempt market in 1981, the program returned to a more traditional form of raising capital, direct investment. Under the Direct Investment Program, the financial institutions lend capital directly to CFI and receive from the Foundation a variable rate of return on a quarterly basis.

The first year that State Escheat Fund income was used to make student loans was in 1973-74, provided through the State Education Assistance Authority.

In 1974-75 CFI became the administrator of the Educational Award Program of the Smith Richardson Foundation.

The following year CFI made its final payment to banks on the original investment for Bankers Student Loans made during the period 1963-66.

The NCBA Student Loan Committee recommended the return to direct funding of student loans between participating banks and CFI. Wachovia Bank and Trust Company agreed to fund the loan program for one year while details for direct funding were worked out with the other banks.

Continuing the rapid growth of student financial assistance programs, the annual dollar volume approached $50 million in 1983-84.

Observing its 30th year of student loan involvement in 1984-85, CFI chalked

CFI President Duffy L. Paul announces cumulative loan and grant approvals in excess of one-half *billion* dollars. His expectations were realized.

up annual program volume of more than $55 million in loans and grants to over 30,000 North Carolina students.

The impressive figures as of June 30, 1989, are: Total financial aid — 349,376 loans and grants to 169,751 students for $554.0 million. Total loan principal repaid — $175.3 million. And total loan principal outstanding — $325.4 million.

One-half billion dollars!

On August 5, 1988, CFI President Duffy L. Paul wrote to the trustees and staff of the Foundation: "With the loan and grant approvals, for 1988-89, mailed to students the week of July 18, CFI exceeded the one-half billion dollar mark in combined cumulative program dollar volume of financial assistance to North Carolina students," he said.

"We have come a long way since 1955-56, the first year of the charter, and 1963-64, the first full year of operation when we made 200 loans totaling $90,000. During the past four fiscal years, our annual program volume has exceeded $50,000,000 to an average of 30,000 students per year and we expect 1988-89 will be the fifth consecutive year that we will exceed that amount," Paul reported. His expectations were realized.

"A special thank you goes to North Carolina banks for their 25 years of funding the loan programs, to the North Carolina State Education Assistance Authority for insuring the loans, and for providing Escheat Loan Funds and Incentive Grant Funds, to special investors, donors, trustees, staff, financial aid administrators, high school counselors and all others involved in our programs of financial assistance for North Carolina students," Paul concluded.

From $90,000 in 1963-64 to $554 million — expansion and filling the student loan needs in North Carolina!

Chapter Eight

Leadership – Practicality and Brainpower

*. . . the study convinced Chairman Bell (NCBA Special Student Loan
Committee) and his fellow committeemen that our plan should be
developed through the vehicle of the College Foundation. . . .*
— *The Tarheel Banker*, December 1962

THE TOTAL STORY OF STUDENT
LOANS in North Carolina through CFI
suggests the title of this book, *The Will and
the Way.*

Its leadership clearly stands out as wise
men and women with liberal amounts of
practicality.

John D. Rockefeller, Jr., said: "The success of each is dependent upon the success
of the other."

By using the vehicle of the College
Foundation and for working to establish
the State Education Assistance Authority,
there was created a classic model for success by wisdom and practicality.

And by turning to Raleigh banker Victor E. Bell, Jr., Governor Terry Sanford
utilized the exceptional capacity of a person
who knew well then and now the rules for
success.

Since 1964 Duffy L. Paul has been the
chief staff executive, and has developed a
professional staff that is widely recognized.
One of the hallmarks of CFI has been the
longevity of service, beginning with Chairman Bell, who has served in that capacity
since July 12, 1962. Trustee Raymond A.
Stone began his membership on the board,
also on July 12, 1962.

CFI Chairman Victor E. Bell, Jr. and Trustee Raymond A. Stone—in service from the beginning.

The following is a list of the members and officers of the Board of Trustees and officers of the Corporation and the dates of their original appointments:

Board Members	Board Officers	Original Appointments
Victor E. Bell, Jr., Chairman Marjan, Inc. Raleigh	Chairman and Chief Executive Officer	July 12, 1962
H. Jack Runnion, Jr. Senior Executive Vice President Wachovia Bank & Trust Co., NA Winston-Salem	Vice Chairman	November 22, 1976
Charles J. Stewart President Guaranty State Bank Durham	Treasurer of the Board and the Corporation	February 8, 1982
James H. Garner Executive Vice President First Bank Troy		October 31, 1987
John J. Godbold, Jr. President Lincoln Bank of NC Lincolnton		July 24, 1987
Robert F. Lowe President Lexington State Bank Lexington		July 24, 1987
Dr. W. Burkette Raper President Mount Olive College Mount Olive		October 4, 1977
Dr. Raymond A. Stone President (Retired) Sandhills Community College Pinehurst		July 12, 1962
Dr. Jewett L. Walker Secretary-Treasurer Brotherhood Pension Service, Inc. A.M.E. Zion Church Charlotte		January 8, 1987

28

Corporation Officers:

Duffy L. Paul President & Chief Staff Executive	Secretary of the Board	August 1, 1964
Gwen P. Davis Senior Vice President & Chief Administrative Officer	Secretary of the Corporation & Assistant Secretary of the Board	January 1, 1971
Norman T. Watson Vice President & Chief Financial Officer	Assistant Secretary & Assistant Treasurer of the Board & the Corporation	October 1, 1966

Bell, Runnion, Stewart and Paul constitute the Executive Committee.

Pictured going clockwise around table: B. Raper; J. Walker; R. Lowe; J. Runnion; V. Bell; D. Paul; C. Stewart; R. Stone; J. Godbold; S. Broadway, executive director, State Education Assistance Authority; G. Davis; and N. Watson. Not pictured: J. Garner.

CFI trustees before charter revision in 1962:

William R. Long, Tarboro	1956-57	1 year
Leonard Powers, Raleigh	1956-57	1 year
Reid Thompson, Pittsboro	1956-57	1 year
Spencer Love, Greensboro	1956-58	2 years
J. Gregory Poole, Raleigh	1956-58	2 years
Phil Whitley, Wendell	1956-58	2 years
R. Mayne Albright, Raleigh	1956-59	3 years
Mrs. Roland McClamroch, Chapel Hill	1956-59	3 years
Terry Sanford, Fayetteville	1956-59	3 years
L. H. Jobe, Raleigh	1956-60	4 years

Former CFI trustees after charter revisions:

Norris L. Hodgkins, Jr., Southern Pines	1962-63	1 year
William L. Archie, Raleigh	1963-65	2 years
Frank H. Kenan, Durham	1963-67	4 years
Lawrence R. Bowers, Whiteville	1983-87	4 years
William H. Stanley, Rocky Mount	1964-69	5 years
James E. Lambeth, Jr., Thomasville	1971-77	6 years
Emsley A. Laney, Wilmington	1968-75	7 years
Clyde L. Stutts, Shelby	1975-82	7 years
R.G. Page, Jr., Winston-Salem	1963-71	8 years
Robert E. Bryan, Goldsboro	1965-75	10 years
Joseph E. Sandlin, Lumberton	1971-83	12 years
John B. Harris, Jr., Raleigh	1975-87	12 years
W.L. Burns, Jr., Durham	1963-76	13 years
Foy N. Goforth, Wilson	1970-87	17 years
Micou F. Browne, Raleigh	1968-86	18 years

The length of service of Chairman Bell and Trustee Stone is a testimonial of their high dedication to volunteer service.

Another impressive record is the longevity of the current staff, headed by President Paul, who began in 1964.

Vivian Schaler, secretary to President Paul, holds a significant record at CFI. Except for Paul, she is the employee with the most years of service — 25 years. When she began her employment at CFI, she was one of only three employees. She is a graduate of Hardbarger Business College, and she has worked as receptionist, payroll clerk, lending supervisor and administrative assistant.

Norman T. Watson, next in length of years, is vice president and chief financial officer. He came to CFI in 1966 when the fledgling organization had a staff of six and annual loan volume of $1 million. He manages the flow of funds, incoming and outgoing. A graduate of Atlantic Christian College, he has a B.A. degree in business administration and is a native of Rocky Mount.

Jo Ann Boyette, general ledger coordinator, joined CFI in 1968. When she began her employment at CFI, she was one of three employees in the area of business and finance. Now she is one of fourteen. She is a native of Raleigh and is a graduate of Hardbarger.

Sharon Roberts, repayment servicing manager, has been an employee of CFI since 1970. Also a graduate of Hardbarger, she has attended evening classes at Wake Community College and Meredith College.

Gwen P. Davis is CFI's senior vice president and chief administrative officer. She joined CFI in 1971. A native of Brevard, she is a *cum laude* graduate of Meredith College. She has been widely recognized for her service on various committees of state and national student financial aid organizations.

Lawrence E. Allen, vice president, program information and grants, began his work at CFI in 1975. He is a native of Raleigh, a graduate of Shaw University with a B.A. degree in business administration. He is a member of the board of trustees of Wake Technical College and has served as vice chariman of the board for eight years.

The first special student loan committee for the North Carolina Bankers Association was headed by Victor E. Bell, Jr., serving during the formation of the Bankers Student Loan Plan and the CFI charter revision. Until 1970, the committee function was handled by the NCBA officers and finance committee. In 1970 Clyde L. Stutts, a Shelby banker, became chairman of the NCBA Student Loan Committee. Other bankers who have headed the committee are: John B. Harris, Jr., Raleigh; H. Jack Runnion, Jr., Winston-Salem; James W. Thompson, Charlotte; and G.B. Carrier, Jr., Charlotte, the current chairman.

George S. Erath, High Point, is chairman of the board of directors of the State Education Assistance Authority. Other members are: Cicero Green, Durham; Ovide E. de St. Aubin, Siler City; John A. Campbell, Charlotte; Mrs. Betty Suttles, Franklin; and Mrs. Paula Rowe Warlick, Lewisville.

Stan C. Broadway continues as the long time executive director and secretary of the board, and Charles F. George, Jr., is associate director and assistant secretary of the board. Both are from Raleigh.

In 1972, with the reorganization of higher education in North Carolina, the Authority became a part of The University of North Carolina. A staff of 41 now occupies offices in the Research Triangle Park and in Raleigh. The Authority is North Carolina's statutory body charged with student aid administration.

Vivian Schaler
(1964)

Norman T. Watson
(1966)

Jo Ann Boyette
(1968)

Sharon Roberts
(1970)

Gwen P. Davis
(1971)

Lawrence E. Allen
(1975)

(Biographical sketches of these CFI employees with long years of service are on page 30.)

Chapter Nine

Headquarters and a Modern Student Loan Facility

Our business is investing in the future—in young people, in students. We wish to make better opportunities for them and for the state.
—VICTOR E. BELL, JR., chairman, CFI Board of Trustees, June 30, 1987, groundbreaking for CFI office building.

THE BIG MOMENT had arrived.

On a sultry June 30, 1987, under a tent on the site, there were approximately 100 persons on hand to witness and applaud the groundbreaking for the new CFI headquarters building in Raleigh at 2100 Yonkers Road near the Beltline and U.S. 1 North.

It was a time for rejoicing and reflection. Soon the York Construction Company of Raleigh would build a new 40,000 square foot building for College Foundation, the sole occupant.

Some recalled the first office of CFI in 1963, a small office in First Citizens Bank in downtown Raleigh with two employees.

CFI Chairman Bell combined expressions of appreciation with an overview of the Foundation's early history. He reminded the audience that "32 years ago Governor Luther Hodges, who had a lifelong dedication to education filed the original certificate of incorporation, thereby establishing the Foundation; 25 years ago Governor Terry Sanford called on North Carolina bankers to establish a state-wide student loan program and offered the Foundation as the vehicle for its administration; the North Carolina Bankers Association ac-

cepted the challenge and has backed and nourished this educational loan program until the current annual loan volume is over $55 million for almost 30,000 students."

He recognized the trustees, CFI's staff, the NCBA Student Loan Committee, the State Education Assistance Authority, the over 300 contributors, including other foundations, college administrators, the guidance counselors in the high schools, the Methodist Conference for the office space it had leased to CFI for a number of years, and students and parents.

Bell singled out two individuals by name and expressed appreciation to the two who "have given daily leadership in the growth of the Foundation over the past 25 years — Duffy Paul, CFI president, and Stan Broadway, executive director of the State Education Assistance Authority."

CFI's office was located from 1963-69 in First Citizens Bank Building in downtown Raleigh; from 1969-73, in the Ruark Building, St. Mary's Street; 1973-88, Methodist Building, 1307 Glenwood Avenue, all in Raleigh.

For some time CFI leaders had felt the

need for greatly expanded space. After careful study, it was decided in 1986 that it would be more practical to purchase land and have a building constructed that would provide for CFI growth for at least 25 years and would be fully efficient.

The new building at 2100 Yonkers Road was occupied on March 21, 1988.

The board of trustees named it the Victor E. Bell, Jr. Building in honor of his more than 25 years of service as CFI chairman.

On November 29, 1988, a large crowd attended an Open House at the Bell Building on the 33rd anniversary of CFI's charter.

Groundbreaking, June 30, 1987, for new CFI office building

Top left: Last minute preparations
Top right: CFI Chairman Victor E. Bell, Jr.
Bottom left: CFI Chairman Bell; J. Willie York, chairman, Board of Directors, York Construction Company; and Raleigh Mayor Avery Upchurch
Bottom right: Stan C. Broadway, executive director, State Education Assistance Authority; CFI Chairman Bell; and CFI President Duffy L. Paul.

Chapter Ten

A Look to the Future and a Continuing Challenge

Education is still the best hope for the future.
—CFI Chairman Victor E. Bell, Jr.

THE DRAMATIC ANNOUNCEMENT in 1988 was that with the loan and grant approvals for 1988-89, CFI exceeded the one-half billion dollar mark in combined cumulative program dollar volume of financial assistance to North Carolina students.

(That amount reached $554 million as of June 30, 1989.)

CFI President Duffy L. Paul announced last year that during the past four fiscal years the annual program volume had exceeded $50 million to an average of 30,000 students per year.

On July 25, 1962, the reconstituted board of trustees convened in Governor Sanford's office. Sanford had surprised Victor E. Bell, Jr., youthful Raleigh banker and civic leader, when he asked him to lead

CFI. At the meeting, Bell was elected chairman of the board, a position he has held since then with skill and a highly positive record of achievement.

It is not possible to accurately calculate the total number of hours he has spent in dedicated leadership to CFI. Soft-spoken, wise, and possessing an admirable blend of humor and sincerity, Chairman Bell continues to be a leader with an inordinate drive to help educate young men and women in North Carolina.

As of June 30, 1989, 169,751 students have been aided by CFI under his leadership.

"Education is still the best hope for the future," he asserts convincingly.

Here is Vic Bell's philosophy as he has set forth in "A Look to the Future."

A Look To The Future

Student financial assistance has become a large, costly and vitally important enterprise in North Carolina and nationwide. Anyone who has been associated with student financial aid for any length of time is struck by how complicated the rules and regulations are and how they, the students and the colleges must deal with a multitude of programs and organizations. Thirty years ago, the few programs available were relatively simple though inadequately funded. In the past ten years, loans have replaced grants and scholarships as the major forms of student aid.

Almost fifty percent of all undergraduate students receive some type of financial aid and student aid pays about sixty percent of college costs. In 1986 student financial aid became a $100 billion dollar business nationwide.

Student financial aid is vitally important because higher education is vitally important. All of us involved in financial aid administration need to remain deeply committed to the principle of equal educational opportunity for all citizens regardless of income level.

Education is still the best hope for the future. As we look ahead to the 21st century, one fact stands out: we need an educated society more than ever. The greatest challenge will be to develop the leadership and means to achieving an educated society. Many low income people see education and job training as vital in overcoming poverty.

Higher education is no longer a luxury for the few, but a necessity for all. In a society which is increasingly dependent on information simply to meet basic needs, like housing, clothing and food, and certainly to meet more complex needs, people with formal education ending at the high school level or even lower will find themselves unable to earn a living, make a life, or relate successfully to other people and the environment.

The future for CFI holds great promise. Need for student financial assistance will increase. True to its past, CFI will respond to this need. It will refine current modes of assistance and seek opportunities to provide new forms of student financial assistance and services.

As college costs continue to rise, North Carolinians will have increased need for educational loans and grants. North Carolina banks stand ready to fund more and larger loans. CFI staff will find additional ways to counsel students about setting limits on the aggregate amounts they borrow. Helping students with debt management will become an increasing priority. The processing of loan and grant applications will become more fully automated, giving CFI staff additional time to deal on a personal basis with students and parents.

I have been impressed with the idea of a general scholarship fund that was advocated by Governor Luther H. Hodges. He was intensely interested in North Carolina's needs for students.

In addition to doing things that are being done today, it seems to me that a general scholarship fund ought to be established, available to North Carolina students to enroll in college and universities of the state. This could be a prestigious special scholarship fund. The good that it would do would be a tremendous boost for scholarship and would stimulate students throughout North Carolina to compete for a scholarship. Governor Hodges foresaw the need for scholarship. He planted the idea, and it seems to me that it would be very good to pursue the idea.

In responding to the challenges and opportunities of the future, CFI staff and trustees with the help of North Carolina banks, the North Carolina State Education Assistance Authority, special investors, donors, financial aid administrators, high school counselors, and many others will continue to do what CFI is all about—people helping people.

> Victor E. Bell, Jr.
> Chairman of the Board
> and Chief Executive Officer
> College Foundation Inc.

North Carolina developed a unique system for student loans beginning in 1955.

For 27 of CFI's 34 years Victor E. Bell, Jr. has contributed his leadership as chairman. Few Tar Heels can claim a much greater public service role — in longevity and effectiveness.

At the outset it was stressed that for a young person in North Carolina who had the skill and the will every effort would be made to find the way.

College Foundation has been successful beyond expectations in helping to make the way a reality.

Through it North Carolina became first in the nation for this unique type of student loan program.

William C. Friday, former president of the University of North Carolina system, said of CFI last year, quoted in *The News and Observer:* "It fills a critical need in North Carolina because we do not even yet have as many of our college-age youth going to school as we should," he said.

Friday said CFI's success is a reflection of the spirit of Mr. Bell and others who have worked for it."I salute Victor Bell because it was tenacity and his sense of uncommon dedication that has sustained the work of the foundation for many years," Friday concluded.

Appendixes

1

CFI Corporate Structure

Incorporators (Certificate of Incorporation - November 29, 1955)

Governor of the State of North Carolina (Luther H. Hodges)
Treasurer of the State of North Carolina (Edwin M. Gill)
Chairman of the State Board of Higher Education (D.H. Ramsey)

Members of the Corporation (Individuals holding these offices)

Governor of the State of North Carolina
Treasurer of the State of North Carolina
Chairman of the Board of Governors of The University of North Carolina

Board of Trustees (Appointed by the Governor)

Five of the nine trustees shall be appointed by the Governor from nominations by the North Carolina Bankers Association. The other four trustees shall be appointed by the Governor to represent the public at large, and shall not be employed by or in any way connected with the banking industry. No persons holding any office by popular election in the government of the State of North Carolina or of the United States shall be eligible to serve as trustees. Only citizens and residents of the State of North Carolina shall be eligible to serve as trustees.

Officers of the Board of Trustees (Elected by the trustees)

Chairman of the Board
Vice Chairman of the Board
Treasurer of the Board and the Corporation
Secretary of the Board
Assistant Secretary
Assistant Treasurer

Executive Committee of the Board of Trustees (Designated by the trustees)

Chairman of the Board
Vice Chairman of the Board
Treasurer of the Board
Secretary of the Board

Officers of the Corporation (Elected by the trustees)

President of the Corporation and Secretary of the Board
Senior Vice President and Secretary of the Corporation
   and Assistant Secretary of the Board
Vice President of the Corporation and Assistant Secretary
   and Assistant Treasurer of the Board and the Corporation

2

CFI Organizational Chart

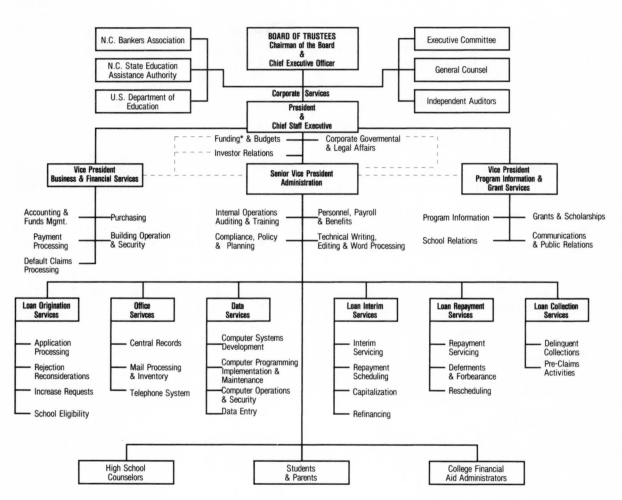

*N.C. Banks & Special Investors
N.C. State Education Assistance Authority

3

CFI Management Staff

Supervisors & Coordinators

Joan Adams
Central Records Supervisor

Cedric Barksdale
Interim Services Supervisor

Laura Barnett
Student Grant Coordinator

Mona Blackwell
Data Entry Supervisor

Jo Ann Boyette
General Ledger Coordinator

Alvin Canton
Payment Processing Coordinator

Sherri Furr
Repayment Servicing Supervisor

Betty Johnson
Pre-Claims Activities Supervisor

Mary Bland Josey
Communications Coordinator

Jacqueline Lynn
Mail & Inventory Supervisor

Ellen Mathis
School Relations Coordinator

Michael McDuffie
Program Information Supervisor

Jean Mertens
Loan Origination Coordinator

Rebecca Rumsey
Personnel & Payroll Coordinator

Rusti Seely
Collection Supervisor

George Travis
Administrative Coordinator

Bonnie Wilkins
Business Servicing Supervisor

Sandy Wolfe
Programming Projects
  Coordinator

Left to right: W. Stice, B. Johnson, D. Paul, V. Bailey, G. Davis, L. Allen, B. Lee, N. Watson, and S. Holz

Senior Management

Duffy L. Paul
President

Norman T. Watson
Vice President
Business & Finance

Gwen P. Davis
Senior Vice President

Lawrence E. Allen
Vice President
Program Information &
  Grants

Service Area Managers

Viola Bailey
Interim Services Manager

Stephanie Holz
Collection Services Manager

Bonnie Johnson
Loan Origination Manager

Betty Lee
Office Services Manager

Sharon Roberts
Repayment Services Manager

William Stice
Data Services Manager

Georgia Thompson
Operations Auditing Manager

39

4

CFI Advisory Committee of Financial Aid Administrators 1988-89

The Advisory Committee of North Carolina Financial Aid Administrators advises the Foundation on items of mutual concern to the financial aid community and the Foundation.

Steven E. Brooks
Dean of Academic Services
Louisburg College
Louisburg

Velma J. Bullock
Financial Aid Administrator
Wake Technical College
Raleigh

Ray Edwards
Director of Financial Aid
East Carolina University
Greenville

John B. Hiott
Director of Scholarships/
    Financial Aid
Meredith College
Raleigh

Eleanor S. Morris
Director of Student Aid
University of North Carolina
    at Chapel Hill
Chapel Hill

James E. Taylor
Student Loan Officer
Elizabeth City State University
Elizabeth City

Ex Officio

Eileen T. Dills
(NCASFAA President)
Director of Financial Aid
Belmont Abbey College
Belmont

Delores S. Davis
(NCASFAA President-elect)
Director of Student Financial Aid
North Carolina A&T State
    University
Greensboro

Stan C. Broadway
Executive Director
North Carolina State
    Education Assistance Authority
Chapel Hill

5

Student Loan Committee North Carolina Bankers Association 1988-89

The North Carolina Bankers Association Student Loan Committee is the funding committee for the educational loan programs administered by College Foundation Inc. as the central leader for North Carolina banks under the nationwide Robert T. Stafford Loan Program (sometimes referred to as the Part B or Guaranteed Student Loan programs).

G. B. Carrier, Jr., Chairman
Executive Vice President
First Union National Bank
Charlotte

H. J. Runnion, Jr., Vice Chairman
Senior Executive Vice President
Wachovia Bank and Trust Co., N.A.
Winston-Salem

Harllee W. Lyon
Senior Vice President
Branch Banking and Trust Co.
Wilson

Morris D. Marley
Executive Vice President
Southern National Bank
Lumberton

C. Nathaniel Siewers
Senior Vice President
Peoples Bank & Trust Co.
Rocky Mount

Craig M. Wardlaw
Executive Vice President
NCNB National Bank
Charlotte

Ex Officio

A.D. Fuqua, Jr.
Executive Vice President
North Carolina Bankers Association
Raleigh

Stan C. Broadway
Executive Director
North Carolina State Education
    Assistance Authority
Chapel Hill

Duffy L. Paul
President
College Foundation Inc.
Raleigh

6

NCBA Student Loan Committee Chairmen

(The first NCBA Special Student Loan Committee was headed by Victor E. Bell, Jr., in 1962, serving during the formation of the Bankers Student Loan Plan and the CFI charter revision. Until 1976, the committee function was handled by the NCBA officers and finance committee. In 1976, Clyde L. Stutts, Shelby banker, began a long tenure as chairman.)

The following is the list of chairmen:

Victor E. Bell, Jr., Raleigh
Clyde L. Stutts, Shelby
John B. Harris, Jr., Raleigh
H. Jack Runnion, Jr., Winston-Salem
James W. Thompson, Charlotte
G.B. Carrier, Jr., Charlotte

7

North Carolina Bankers Association

Presidents since 1962 when CFI was restructured and the Bankers Student Loan Program was announced:

Oscar J. Mooneyham, Forest City; John J. Mason, Tarboro; Robert P. Holding, Jr., Smithfield; Clyde L. Stutts, Shelby; Emsley A. Laney, Wilmington; W. Charles Barrett, Laurinburg; J. Paul Ford, Belmont; W. H. Stanley, Rocky Mount; Bland W. Worley, Winston-Salem; Claude C. Armfield, Jr., Asheville; Lawrence R. Bowers, Whiteville; Claude Henson, Asheboro; Hugh L. McColl, Jr., Charlotte; James B. Powers, Rocky Mount; John F. McNair III, Winston-Salem; John A. Forlines, Jr., Granite Falls; H.L. Ruth, Jr., Concord; W.L. Burns, Jr., Durham; Plato Pearson, Jr., Gastonia; Thorne Gregory, Wilson; Ben T. Craig, North Wilkesboro; Theodore B. Sumner, Jr., Charlotte; John B. Harris, Jr., Raleigh; Francis B. Kemp III, Charlotte; Paul E. Fisher, Granite Quarry; L. Glenn Orr, Jr., Lumberton; E. Rhone Sasser, Whiteville; L. Vincent Lowe, Jr., Wilson; and James M. Culberson, Jr., Asheboro.

Managing Officers of the NCBA since CFI was restructured:
Harry Gatton and Alvah D. Fuqua, Jr., both of Raleigh.

CFI General Counsel:
Bailey and Dixon*

Independent Auditors:
Koonce Wooten and Haywood

*In the structuring of the student loan bonds and the court tests Attorney Kenneth F. Wooten, now retired, provided invaluable legal advice.

8

North Carolina State Education Assistance Authority

Board of Directors:

George S. Erath, chairman, High Point; Mrs. Betty Suttles, vice chairman, Franklin; Ovide E. de St. Aubin, treasurer, Siler City; Leslie M. Baker, Winston-Salem; Dr. Ida Fay Caudle Byrd, Roaring River; James W. Perkins, Greensboro; and Mrs. Paula Rowe Warlick, Lewisville.

Former Members of Board of Directors:

Edwin C. Baker, Raleigh; Victor E. Bell, Jr., Raleigh; William L. Burns, Jr., Durham; John A. Campbell, Charlotte; Mrs. Willie Dorman, Fayetteville; Thomas J. Elijah, Jr., Pfafftown; Richard Futrell, Rocky Mount; Steve Gabriel, Boone; Roger Gant, Jr., Glen Raven Mills; Cicero Green, Durham; Benton T. Haithcock, Mount Gilead; Mrs. Carrie W. Harper, Greensboro; J. Russell Kirby, Wilson; Watts Hill, Jr, Chapel Hill; W.H. Plemmons, Boone; W. Burkette Raper, Mount Olive; Mrs. Julia Wheeler Taylor, Durham; C. Richard Vaughn, Mount Airy; D. Douglas Wade, Jr., Rocky Mount; Arthur D. Wenger, Wilson; and H. Edmunds White, Davidson.

Past Chairmen of the Board:

Watts Hill, Jr., J. Russell Kirby, Edwin C. Baker and Richard Futrell.

Management Staff:

Stan C. Broadway, Executive Director (1966-present)
Charles F. George, Jr., Associate Director (1970-present)

9

CFI Educational Loan Fund Investors
1963 - 1989

American Bank & Trust Co.
American Defender Life Insurance Co.
Asheboro College
Atlantic Christian College
Avery County Bank
Babcock Graduate School of Management
   of Wake Forest University
Bank of Alamance
Bank of Asheville
Bank of Belmont
Bank of Candor
Bank of Conway

Bank of Currituck
Bank of Eden
Bank of Four Oaks
Bank of Granite
Bank of Iredell
Bank of Montgomery
Bank of North Carolina
Bank of Pilot Mountain
Bank of Pine Level
Bank of Raeford
Belmont Abbey College
Branch Banking & Trust Co.

Brevard College
Broyhill Family Foundation, Inc.
James E. & Mary Z. Bryan Foundation, Inc.
Burlington National Bank
Byrum-Mansfield Memorial Student Loan Fund
Cabarrus Bank & Trust Co.
Campbell University
Cape Fear Bank
Capitol National Bank
Carolina Bank
Carolina First National Bank
Carolina State Bank
Central Carolina Bank, N.A.
Central State Bank
Cherryville National Bank
Chowan College
Citizens Bank
Citizens National Bank
City National Bank
Clayton High School
Columbus National Bank
Commercial & Farmers Bank
Commercial & Savings Bank
Community Bank of Carolina
Concord National Bank
County Bank & Trust Co.
Cumberland Bank
Dayco Credit Union
James W. Denmark Loan Fund of
    Wake Forest University
Duke University Federal Credit Union
East Carolina Bank
Edgecombe Bank & Trust Co.
Elon College
Farmers Bank
Farmers & Merchants Bank
Fidelity Bank
First Bank
First Charter National Bank
First Citizens Bank & Trust Co.
First Community Bank
First National Bank of Albemarle
First National Bank of Anson County
First National Bank of Catawba County
First National Bank of Randolph County
First National Bank of Reidsville
First National Bank of Shelby
First State Bank
First Union National Bank of N.C.
Forsyth Bank & Trust Co.
Gardner-Webb College
Gateway Bank
Greensboro College
Greensboro National Bank
Guaranty State Bank
Hardbarger Junior College of Business

Heritage Bank
High Point College
Independence National Bank
Kemp Furniture Industries, Inc.
Lafayette Bank & Trust Co.
Lees-McRae College
Lenoir-Rhyne College
Lexington State Bank
Liberty Bank & Trust Co.
Lincoln Bank of N.C.
Louisburg College
Mechanics & Farmers Bank
Merchants & Farmers Bank
Meredith College
MetroBank, N.A.
Mid-South Bank & Trust Co.
Mount Olive College
N.C. Mutual Life Insurance Co.
N.C. State Board of Registration for Professional
    Engineers and Land Surveyors
N.C. State Education Assistance Authority
N.C. State Firemen's Association
NCNB National Bank
Northwestern Bank
Peace College
Peoples Bank
Peoples Bank & Trust Co.
Peoples Bank of N.C.
Piedmont Aerospace Institute
Piedmont Bank & Trust Co.
Planters Bank
Randolph Bank & Trust Co.
Republic Bank & Trust Co.
Richmond County Bank
St. Andrews Presbyterian College
St. Augustine's College
St. Mary's College
Salem College
Security Bank & Trust Co.
Southern Bank & Trust Co.
Southern National Bank of N.C.
State Bank of Raleigh
State Employees' Credit Union
Tarheel Bank & Trust Co.
Telco Credit Union of Asheville
Town & Country Bank
Triangle Bank & Trust Co.
Union National Bank
United Carolina Bank
United Citizens Bank
United National Bank
Waccamaw Bank & Trust Co.
Wachovia Bank & Trust Co., N.A.
Western Carolina Bank
Wingate College
Yadkin Valley Bank & Trust Co.

10

CFI Donors, 1955 - 1989

A.T. Adams
Fred H. Allen
Mr. & Mrs. Gordon P. Allen
American Defender Life Ins. Co.
American Trust Company
Asheville Citizen-Times Co.
Aviation Fuel Terminals
N.E. Aydlett
Mary Reynolds Babcock
    Foundation, Inc.
Sara McIntyre Bahner
William H. Barnhardt
Mrs. Thomas H. Battle Estate
Mrs. Louise T. Beam
Bear, Stearns & Co.
Belk Stores
Mr. and Mrs. Victor E. Bell, Jr.
Edward B. Benjamin Estate
Robert J. Benson, Jr.
Jennie Schneider Bern
Mrs. James Blackburn
Alyce F. Blanton
C.D. Blalock
Blue Bell, Inc.
Blue Ridge Trucking Company
Franklin J. Blythe, Jr.
Richard N. Blythe
A.G. Boone Co.
Boren Clay Products, Inc.
Bost's Bakery, Inc.
Branch Banking & Trust Co.
Mrs. Kedar S. Brown
Mary B. Brown
James E. & Mary Z. Bryan
    Foundation Inc.
Kathleen Price & Joseph M.
    Bryan Family Foundation, Inc.
R.A. Bryan
R.A. Bryan Foundation, Inc.
Sarah Booth Bryan
Burlington Industries
    Foundation, Inc.
Business Development
    Corporation of N.C.
Bruce B. Cameron
Daniel D. Cameron
Cameron Village, Inc.
Charles A. Cannon
Martin Cannon Family
    Foundation, Inc.
Carolina Power & Light Co.
Carolina Steel Corp.
Carolina Tel. & Tel. Co.
Carolina Tire & Retreading Co.

Carteret-Craven Electric
    Membership Corp.
Central Carolina Bank &
    Trust Co.
Central Engineering Co.
Mary Chambers
Chatham Foundation, Inc.
Robert E. Cline
Citizens National Bank
Collier Cobb, Jr.
Collier Cobb, III
Alan W. Cone
Benjamin Cone
Herman Cone, Jr.
Lenox G. Cooper
W. Dunlop Covington
Betty Condruff Craig
Caroline Taylor Craig
Cromartie Transport Co.
W.R. Cuthbertson
W.Reynolds Cuthbertson, Jr.
E.A. Dalrumple
H.M. Dalton
Mrs. Sidney E. Daniels
Roy W. Davis, Jr.
R.L. Deal
Dillon Supply Co.
William A. Dixon, Jr.
Duke Power Co.
East Carolina Bank
Ernest O. Edwards
E. Hervey Evans
Farmer's Hardware & Supply
James S. Ficklen, Jr.
Thomas P. Ficklen
Fidelity Bank
Nancy Hodges Finley
A.E. Finley
A.E. Finley & Associates, Inc.
First-Citizens Bank & Trust Co.
First Union National Bank
Forbes Transfer Co.
Mrs. Anne G. Foster
Edythe Fowler
Robert H. Francis
Martha McCoy Fulton
Roger T. Gant, Jr.
R. Walker Geitner
Globe Furniture Co.
Horton E. Gragg
Sam T. Gresham, Jr.
Mrs. Edward Haley
Frank P. Hall, Jr.
C. Rush Hamrick, Jr.

Hanes Dye & Finishing Co.
Charles P. Hanrahan, Jr.
Dr. & Mrs. A. Page Harris
James J. Harris
R.L. Harris, Jr., Heirs
W.H. Harris, III, Heirs
Lallah W. Heath
Paul J. Helms
Hemby Investments, Inc.
George Watts Hill
J.S. Hill
J.S. Hill, Jr.
Governor Luther H. Hodges
Luther H. Hodges, Jr.
George Hoff
Homes Security Life Ins. Co.
Julia B. Humphrey
Independence National Bank
Challis T. Isley
Jefferson Standard Life Ins. Co.
Halbert M. Jones
E.M. Kearns Estates, Inc.
Frank H. Kenan
Kent-Coffey Foundation, Inc.
King Roofing & Mfg. Co.
Susan McCoy Kinlaw
Marvin B. Koonce, Jr.
Dianne Sumner Lambeth
Lance, Inc.
Emsley A. Laney
Lee Brick & Tile Co.
Lee-Moore Oil Co.
J. Van Lindley
Mark M. Lindsay
Dr. H.O. Lineberger, Jr.
H.W. Little & Company
Mrs. Bert B. Lloyd
Wilbur R. Lloyd
T.A. Loving Co.
Harold Makepeace
Howard E. Manning, Sr.
H.A. Marks
Ina Walker McCoy
Mary Franklin Jones McCoy
R.F. McCoy
Mrs. R.F. McCoy
Sarah Dabney Little McElroy
Dalton L. McMichael
P.D. Midyette, Jr.
Mobil Oil Co., Inc.
Caroline R. Mock
B.C. Moore & Sons
James L. Morgan
Fred Morrison

Elizabeth D. Murray
John C. Muse
Albert G. Myers, Jr.
Myrtle Desk Co.
Nantahala Power & Light Co.
Natcom & Co.
Nello Teer Co.
The News & Observer
  Publishing Co.
James L. Newsome
N.C. Independent Telephone
  Assoc.
N.C. Natural Gas Corp.
N.C. Products, Inc.
Mrs. Marion Craig Nifong
North State Motor Lines, Inc.
North State Telephone Co.
Mrs. Gertrude J. O'Dowd
Overnite Transportation
  Company
A. Lloyd Owens
Z.V. Pate, Inc.
Amy Cotter Pender
Peoples Bank & Trust Co.
Piedmont Gas Co.
Pilot Life Insurance Co.
Richard S. Pindell
Pine Hall Brick & Pipe Co., Inc.
Pipe, Inc.
Planters National Bank &
  Trust Co.
W.H. Plemmons
Dr. Robert C. Pope
Mrs. Robert E. Porter
Rosa Little Porter
J.A. Prevost
Thomas P. Pruitt
RS&H of North Carolina Inc.
Emily B. Ragsdale
Raleigh Kiwanis Club
Raleigh Office Supply Co.

Mary Wilson Ralph
Mrs. W.F. Redding, III
Evelyn K. Reed
Addison H. Reese
Mrs. John M. Reeves
Rexham Corp.
R.J. Reynolds Co.
Z. Smith Reynolds Foundation,
  Inc.
E. N. Richards
Smith Richardson
  Foundation, Inc.
Alma W. Rivers Trust
Mary McCoy Rivers
J.C. Roberts, III
Mrs. D.W. Robertson, Jr.
Pearl S. Robinson
Catherine R. Robson
Dorothy R. Rogers
Eugene W. Rose
Margaret P. Russell
Ryder Truck Lines, Inc.
Jean R. Scaglion
Jean W. Schenck
Katherine Harris Schloss
Mr. & Mrs. Norden B. Schloss
Sears, Roebuck & Co.
Security National Bank
Selig Manufacturing Co.
Service Printing Co.
A.M. Sharpe
J.A. Sharpe, Jr.
Shell Oil Co.
W. Roland Simpson
Earl F. Slick
Dr. Foyell Smith
Scott H. Smith Estate
Mrs. John K. Snipes
Southeastern Fire Insurance Co.
Southern Bell Telephone Co.
Southern National Bank of N.C.

Mrs. William G. Spencer, Jr.
O.E. Starnes, Jr.
Superior Block Co.
Superior Stone Co.
E. Hoover Taft, Jr.
G. Stanton Taylor
H. Patrick Taylor, Jr.
Bob Timberlake
Elizabeth J. Todd
S.S. Toler & Son
Stella Anderson Trapp
Travelers Oil Co., Inc.
Elmer Troutman
H. J. Truett
United Carolina Bank
T.A. Upchurch
U.S. Fidelity & Guaranty Co.
J.R. Veach, Jr.
Wachovia Bank & Trust
  Co., N.A.
Wade Properties
Clarence S. Wagner
Waldensian Bakeries
Mrs. Courtney Sharpe Ward
Jack Wardlaw
Lawrence A. Watts, Jr.
Wayne Foundation
Gradie J. Wheeler
E.L. White, Jr.
Wilkinson, Bullock & Co.
Alfred Williams & Co.
John A. Williams
Sara B. Williams
Mrs. Faye Chambers Willis
Iva Dean Winkler
Mrs. Oleta Wilson
W.R. Winkler
Yadkin, Inc.
J.W. York

11

CFI Funding Sources

Student and Parent Loan Programs under the Higher Education Act of 1965, As Amended

Bond Funds - Proceeds from the sale of tax-exempt revenue bonds or bond anticipation notes issued by the N.C. State Education Assistance Authority. North Carolina banks purchased the bonds and notes. (Student loans only) (1968-1982)

Direct Funds - North Carolina banks provide funds directly to the Foundation or purchase loans made by the Foundation from advance commitments. (Student and parent loans) (1982 - present)

Escheat Funds - Unclaimed, abandoned or uninherited property that passes to the custody of the State of North Carolina. The N.C. State Education Assistance Authority provides income on the investment of the escheat funds to the Foundation. (Students attending North Carolina public institutions only.) (1973 - present)

Special Funds - North Carolina financial institutions, educational institutions and other organizations provide funds directly to the Foundation. In most cases, the borrower has a special relationship to the provider of funds. (Student and parent loans) (1967 - present)

State Student Incentive Grant Program (SSIG)
The N.C. State Education Assistance Authority provides funds from State and Federal appropriations on a dollar for dollar matching basis. (Students attending North Carolina institutions only.) (1975 - present)

James E. and Mary Z. Bryan Foundation Program
Funds allocated by the Bryan Foundation from income on the investment of the estates of James E. and Mary Zealy Bryan provide funds for Special Scholarships (Goldsboro and Hobbton High School students only.) (1968 - present)

General Operating and Building and Equipment Funds
The various programs the Foundation administers provide the income to cover general operating expenses and other expenses either through service fees or from the spread between borrowing and lending rates.

Donors

Donors are organizations, foundations, trust funds, business, industry, and individuals that make donations to help strengthen the financial base of the Foundation. The Foundation includes a list of donors in its annual report.

Investors

Investors are North Carolina banks, life insurance companies, credit unions, educational institutions, associations, organizations, and other foundations that provide funds for educational loans. The Foundation includes a list of investors in its annual report.

12

Loan and Grant Programs

College Foundation Inc. administers several types of loans and grants. A summary is given below.

- **Loans under the Robert T. Stafford Student Loan Program** (in North Carolina, named the N.C. Insured Student Loan Program) provided for in Title IV of the Higher Education Act of 1965, as amended—

  –Stafford Loans for Students (formerly GSL)
  These low-interest, long-term loans are made to:
    - •• North Carolina students attending eligible institutions of higher education and vocational schools in state and out of state;
    - •• Out-of-state students attending eligible institutions of higher education and vocational schools in North Carolina;
    - •• Graduate as well as undergraduate students.

  –Supplemental Loans for Students (SLS)
  These loans are part of the new Supplemental Loans for Students, established by the Congress in 1986 to replace the ALAS Loans or PLUS Loans to students. Students do not have to demonstrate financial need for this assistance. The loans may be used in addition to the Stafford Loans.

  –PLUS Loans to Parents (PLUS)
  The Foundation administers this program of long-term loans to North Carolina residents who are parents of dependent undergraduate students or to parents of dependent undergraduate students who are attending an eligible North Carolina college, university, technical or vocational school. These loans may be used in addition to the Stafford Loans.

  "General Funds" come from the N.C. SEAA (Escheat Funds) and from banks throughout North Carolina.

  "Special Loan Funds" are made available by North Carolina colleges, universities, technical and vocational schools, financial institutions, and other organizations which wish to provide funds to make available loans to students who might not otherwise be able to get loans (primarily those who do not demonstrate eligibility for the federal interest subsidy).

- **North Carolina Student Incentive Grant Program (N.C. SIG)**

  The Foundation administers this program which is based on substantiated financial need to undergraduate students who are legal residents of North Carolina and who are or will be enrolled in an eligible school in North Carolina.

- **James E. and Mary Z. Bryan Foundation, Inc. - Special Scholarships**

  College Foundation administers the special scholarships program for the Bryan Foundation. This program is available to graduating seniors at Goldsboro and Hobbton High School who are deserving and demonstrate unusual or creative talent in their interest areas.

- **Special Fund Program**

  The Foundation administers this program for North Carolina colleges, universities, technical or vocational schools, financial institutions, and other organizations which wish to invest their funds and receive a return while providing loans to students and parents who might not otherwise be able to get loans.

  –Smith Richardson Foundation, Inc. - Special Donor
  College Foundation makes special student loans from funds donated by the Smith Richardson Foundation under the North Carolina Insured Student Loan Program.

  –Byrum-Mansfield Memorial Student Loan Fund - Special Investor
  College Foundation is the court-appointed trustee for this fund and makes loans under the North Carolina Insured Student Loan Program. Funds are available to needy, qualified students seeking education beyond high school. Preference is given to relatives of Mamie Mansfield, members of Asbury United Methodist Church, and residents of Durham County.

  –Broyhill Family Foundation, Inc. - Special Investor
  College Foundation administers educational loans for the Broyhill Family Foundation under the North Carolina Insured Student Loan Program. Loan funds are available for deserving undergraduate students attending Appalachian State University, Gardner-Webb College, Lees-McRae College, Lenoir-Rhyne College, Mars Hill College, Wake Forest University, and Warren Wilson College.

Index

50

(For the listing of CFI educational loan fund investors, see pages 42-43; for CFI donors, pages 44-45.)